Permission Granted:
The Journey from Trauma to Healing
from Rape, Sexual Assault and Emotional Abuse

Permission Granted:
The Journey from Trauma to Healing
from Rape, Sexual Assault and Emotional Abuse

Kathleen carterMartinez, Ed.D.

Kathleen carterMartinez, Ed.D.

Permission Granted:
The Journey from Trauma to Healing from Rape, Sexual Assault & Emotional Abuse
Kathleen carterMartinez, Ed.D.

CheyWind Center for Trauma and Healing • NY

Published by CheyWind Center for Trauma
ISBN:-13: 978-0692584972

Disclaimer

The information provided in this book is designed to provide helpful information on the subjects discussed. This book is designed to provide information and motivation to our readers. It is sold with the understanding that the publisher is not engaged to render any type of psychological, legal, or any other kind of professional advice.

This book is not meant to be used, nor should it be used, to diagnose or treat any medical or mental health condition. For diagnosis or treatment of any medical or mental health problem, consult your own physician. Neither the publisher nor the individual author(s) shall be liable for any physical, psychological, emotional, financial, or commercial damages, including, but not limited to, special, incidental, consequential or other damages. Our views and rights are the same: You are responsible for your own choices, actions, and results.

Whispers

I have Heard

I have heard of your sorrow
I have heard of your loss
I stand by you...

My heart is on the ground

Kc carterMartinez, Ed.D.

Dedication

This book is dedicated to the 35 women of *The Sorrowful Sisterhood* who had the courage to come forward and give a voice to their own personal traumas in the July 2015 edition of the New York Magazine. This book is also dedicated to all of the voices represented by the empty chair that have come forward since that time in an effort to give a voice to the stories of their own personal traumas.

Permission Granted serves as a reminder to women of *The Sorrowful Sisterhood* and women everywhere that you are not alone.

Permission Granted offers support and acknowledges the immense courage of heart and spirit that it takes to give a voice to one's personal trauma.

As a community of compassionate listeners, we respect and honor your choice to speak at the moment that feels safe and comfortable for you.

For those women who find sanctuary in silence and wish to refrain from giving a voice to their trauma, as members of your community of compassionate listeners we respect your choices and stand by you in supportive silence.

To those who would ask the question: Did this happen to you?

The consistent mantra throughout this book resonates from the first page to the last: The answer does not matter! Any other answer deprives each and every one of us of the benefit and blessing of someone who is willing to listen, the first step in the healing process.

The Lotus

*W*hen we are lost, we constantly look for ways to find our way back home. In the wake of a personal trauma this is almost impossible to do. We are lost, we are confused and we are hurt. Very often we feel as if we are alone, and we are.

Because this way of being is so unbearable, we begin looking outside of ourselves for signs from anyone to help us find our way home. Still, we find ourselves frozen in this painful way of being, not one step closer to being away from our pain or to where we want to be.

In Buddhism, the Lotus represents rebirth, the ability to renew oneself every day. Every evening in all of it's splendor and beautiful colors, the lotus sinks into muddy water where it's beauty becomes submerged and hidden from sight.

Each and every morning, the lotus rises to the surface where once again everyone can witness its beauty and brilliance.

Much the same as the lotus, this book serves as a guide to expand our awareness about the amazing resiliency of the human condition, the mind-body-spirit and our ability to renew and restore ourselves time and time again even in the face of painful personal trauma.

Table of Contents

Dedication

The Lotus

Personal Gratitude

Creative Acknowledgments

Prologue

Where I Fall by: Roy Hurd: Adirondack Singer/Songwriter

Forward

Introduction

Personal Gratitude

*T*here are people who are essential to the very core of our heart that stay with us whatever we do and wherever we go. These are my people, both here and there. It's never enough to just say thank you…

My beloved husband Richard
Who gave me the gift of faith
My inspiration ~ spiritual companion
My one true believer ~ the champion of my heart
The depth of love for which there are no words

My Parents
R.L. and Patsy
Towers of strength
Unconditional love and support
Both here and there
The depth of love for which there are no words

My Daughters
Shanzy and Kasaydia
The greatest gifts of my life
My heart of hearts
The depth of love for which there are no words

My beloved sisters
Patti and Margie
Always one of three
Both here and there — forever
Pinky promise...

My spirit sister Dana
Always family
The calm voice in the storm
Creative powers that light up the dark
Without her
We would not be here

My niece's Melissa and Vanessa
The Memory Keepers
Together they know what it means to keep the faith

My Grandmother Terry
who gave me the gift of telling

My Aunt Helen
who gave me the gift of listening

My Grandparents
Jack and Dorothy
Who gave me the gift of family

Patti & John
Both then and now & here and there
Thank you for all the love & the memories
For the second home
For every kindness
I will keep the light on in the window

Creative Acknowledgments

Dana Filipone
Book cover and interior design

Alyson Levy, MA
Creative Editorial Services

Kasaydia Carter-Martinez, BS
Social Media/Public Relations Manger
Free Lance Videographer

Shanzy Carter-Martinez, MS, MHC, NCC
Artistic Communications Manager
Behavioral Health Consultant

Roy Hurd: Hurdsongs Music
Gifted Courtesy: Where I Fall
Facebook: https://www.facebook.com/public/Roy-Hurd

Misumi Ya'ara Goldman: Designer
Gifted: Calligraphy
Facebook: https://www.facebook.com/
Misumis-Studio-156649424416011/?pnref=lhc

Kathleen carterMartinez, Ed.D.

Prologue

Trauma and Healing - The Journey Home

When it comes to trauma and healing from personal traumas such as rape, sexual assault, and emotional abuse we have to stop asking the question: *Did this happen to you?* The answer is not really important; the fact that you are here is what matters. This book is written in the collective voice of *We* because it is written for each and everyone one of us. We do not ask you to identify if you are a *victim* of a traumatic event or if you are the friend or loved one of someone who has been in harm's way; all are welcome here.

Trauma is trauma. One way or the other we are all part of the healing journey. We do not ask you to qualify to be here to read this book for it is written for all of us. Why is this? Because we are all a member of the human condition and we all sit side-by-side in the circle of healing. What affects one of us ~ affects all of us! All that is asked when you come here, is that you are ready to listen with an open heart and have a shoulder to lean on.

For anyone that has a story to tell but does not wish to give a voice to their story, perhaps not now, perhaps not ever, we understand and honor your choice. When you are ready, *you* have a place here with all of us in the circle of healing. And if all you need is a shoulder to lean on and a safe place to rest your troubled heart, you will find it here in the circle of compassionate listeners.

For anyone who has a story that they wish to give a voice to, this is your time... this is *your* moment...*your* community sits ready to listen.

Follow the path of the healing journey for it is a linear circle. Remember you do not walk alone on this path as we all walk side by side. Together we will follow the path of the linear circle for it will bring us home to the circle of healing.

Now, let us begin the journey to healing.

Where I Fall

Standing at the crossroads love lost
Wondering which way to go
There's so much about love that I just don't know
Robert Johnson made his deal here
His soul for the cool way he played
True love is the one thing the devil can't trade

There is no limit to what I would give a way
The miles I'd travel or the price I'd pay
To have what most of us want most of all
I have searched for love to no avail
I am not afraid to try and fail
I somehow remain hopeful through it all
I make my stand where I fall

I consider all my choices
I can't go back the way I came
The things that got me here I know will never change
We've all had our share of heartbreak
I guess that is just the way it goes
There's bound to be some heartache
Found down any road

There is no limit to what I would give away
The miles I'd travel or the price I'd pay
To have what most of us want most of all
I have searched for love to no avail
I am not afraid to try and fail

I somehow remain hopeful through it all
I make my stand where I fall
Through it all
I make my stand where I fall

'Where I Fall'
Permission and courtesy of Mr. Roy Hurd
Artist: Adirondack Singer/Song Writer/Hurdsongsmusic

Kathleen carterMartinez, Ed.D.

Foreword

Early on, I came to understand that I was born into the aftermath of trauma on my father's side of the family. Long before we had the words to even explain what a traumatic event was, trauma had taken up residence in his family and in his heart, and it never went away.

When families lose their loved ones to extraordinary circumstances and losses, they are never the same. When unimagined traumatic events and losses become part of the family tapestry, the threads of those events wrap themselves around the hearts and memories of those that are left. And no matter how many years have passed, the sorrow of the unexplainable remained in the home and hearts of my loved ones.

Throughout my father's life, he carried a deep, overwhelming sadness in his heart that was reflected in his eyes, like a shadow that never went away.

Over the years, I learned to watch my father from a distance, and I could see when the aftermath of trauma was upon him again. He had a trait best described as a twitch that you could not miss, as he would randomly clench his fist and at the same time jerk his left shoulder back as his jaw would suddenly tighten seemingly without reason and he would have a far-off look in his eyes.

For a moment, it would look as if he were briefly annoyed at something that no one else could see or understand, but nothing could be further from the truth.

At these moments, despite how it looked, he was not annoyed, he was simply haunted by the sorrow that trauma had brought into his life, and the aftermath of trauma had once again come to close. But I came to understand that this was his way of pushing the aftermath of trauma away when once more it was coming to close again. Thus, over time, his sorrow and his story became part of my patchwork tapestry.

From the time that I was old enough to listen, my life was filled with stories about family members that had already crossed over, who were lost too soon to the unexplainable. My grandmother and my aunt would tell me story after story about my grandfather and my uncles that were already gone in such a way that it became routine for me to become engrossed in conversations about family members that were no longer with us as if they were sitting in the kitchen.

From the Beginning

From the very beginning at a tender young age, I learned that it was the telling of and listening to the stories which provided the only healing balm that I have ever known to work on the heart of my grandmother, aunt, and father.

Even though I knew all of these stories by heart, it was the re-telling of them that taught me about the power of the spoken word. For every time they told their stories, their faces became softer; their eyes misted over, and their hearts seem to become lighter.

For that brief moment, I felt and saw what the comfort of spoken words and memories could do to quiet the pain of trauma that never leaves. Each time, I experienced what it meant to be in the presence of those that I have known my entire life, yet have never met.

Having grown up with both my paternal and maternal grandmothers, it was the contrast between their two households wherein I discovered the presence of trauma in my father's family.

The two families were very different. My maternal grandparents' home was deeply rooted in the here and now, the present moment. Their home itself was a reflection of all of the family members that lived in that house at the time and there were very few conversations about family members that were no longer with us.

My paternal grandmother's home, on the other hand, was in stark contrast to this as the home itself looked and felt as if it was stuck in time, but in a very warm and inviting way.

Throughout the house were bits and pieces of things that belonged to other family members who had crossed over many moons ago, and yet here they were in this home. It always seemed as if these family members had merely stepped out and would be back momentarily; I didn't think a thing of it, in fact, it seemed that I was waiting for their return as well. And at times when I was alone in the house, I was never afraid. I knew that I was never alone.

Surprisingly at a very young age, I could see and feel how comforting these rituals and telling's were for my grandmother. And yet, to me, it seemed and felt very normal.

It would be many years later before I would realize that I had made friends with trauma as a young girl, and was not driven to hide from it nor to run away from it. It was simply part of my family, and it felt quite normal to me.

Heart of a Teller

My father embraced the ways of his mother. Although he probably would disagree, he too had the heart of the teller. His sorrow ran very deep, and he preferred to bear it privately.

Although there were times he looked like a bull in a china shop, driven by something that no one could see and very few could understand, I came to know that the aftermath of trauma was upon him again.

It was from my father that I learned about the aftermath of trauma and how once it finds you, it is always with you.

Together we learned that while trauma may take up residence in your heart, your spirit has the power to make a choice, to do something differently to find a peaceful way to co-exist with a resident that refuses to leave.

My father's journey was a very long one; but one day in his later elder years, long after trauma first took up residence in his mind and his heart, he called me at home and said: 'Hey pal, you are never going to believe what I learned today!'

Of course, I had to ask, and this is what he said: 'Do you know that I have been angry for 40 years?'

He had spent hours talking with a trusted spiritual advisor, who somehow found a way to say 'It is ok to put the trauma to rest now. It is ok to make peace with your anger and your sorrow. You don't have to be angry anymore.'

More or less, these are the words that he shared with me years after trauma had first taken up residence in his life, he was finally ready to hear these words.

When my father was with my family, the teller within him would come alive. My dad had a warm affection for my husband. The deep connection that they shared came to life when my father was here with us, in the mountains, the place that we both called home.

Here, my dad was known to sit quietly with my husband and share his stories of tragedy, loss, laughter and loved ones no longer with us. My husband would call our daughters in to come and sit around the table, to listen to Grandpa's telling. Every time my father would look at my husband and say 'Hey, did I ever tell you about the time...?' My husband would say,

'No! Go ahead and tell that one!'

These were beautiful, magical moments because they only came in the very early morning hours or later evening hours. Whenever we heard him say, 'Did I ever tell you about' we all pulled a chair up and sat around while listening to the same stories as if it were for the very first time we were hearing them.

My dad would pull his chair in and look over at me and say 'Hey pal, would you get me a Pepsi, I have a story to tell.'

It Never Occurred to Me ~ A Brother's Sorrow

Years later, quite unexpectedly my father drove all the way up to the mountains to see me one day to talk about my sister. He came in and just sat there motionless as he struggled to find the words to describe how he felt about my sister losing her battle with mental and emotional illness.

When he looked up, all I could see were the tears in his eyes and the years of sorrow he had already carried with him and the profound sadness when he said: 'You know what we are looking at here, don't you?' For my father who had lost one of his brothers to the same powerful adversary, he felt it in his bones that it was just a matter of time until trauma found our family once again.

During his illness, my uncle was hospitalized many times, and for the duration of these episodes, he lost touch with who he was, never mind who anyone else was.

The most painful of these moments were when my father would come for visitation, and my uncle would refuse to speak to him, deny their brotherhood and order him to leave. My Dad never left. Instead, he went to every visitation and sat at the foot of his bed until the visiting time was over, and then returned for the next one.

My father would tell me he knew that trauma was there all along, and that was why he refused to leave his brother. By this time in his life, he had already lost his younger brother, and his father to traumatic events and he would tell me, it never occurred to him to not fight to hold on to the only brother he had left.

So he said that he would sit on the end of that bed and whisper out loud: 'I'm not going anywhere so you might as well sit down'; I asked if he was talking to his brother and he said; 'No, I was talking to *him*!

He did not use the phrase trauma back then, my dad talked about *him or it* and would say things like 'don't let him get you ~ you have to be strong!' It was not until much later in his life that he understood that the aftermath of trauma had taken up residence in his heart, mind and family.

During each hospitalization when my uncle would regain his psychological and spiritual balance, the first and only person he wanted to see was my father, his brother, this is the heartbreak of spiritual and emotional illness.

When my uncle lost his twenty-year battle with mental and emotional illness, the only way that they could identify his body when they found him was by the picture in the wallet that was left open lying next to him. It was a picture of my father.

Wee Hours of Darkness ~ A Sister's Sorrow

This book was written in the wee hours of darkness.
The words that you find here did not see daylight until the very end.

Work like this does not lend itself to the daylight, to sunlight. Instead, it comes to life in the shadows of the evening hours and lingers through the night.

The only daytime hours these pages ever saw, were the days of the misty rain or foggy snow when the spirit walkers came to visit, my favorite time of all.

The spirit walkers come down through the clouds and travel in the fog, through the mountains to the water, and if you wait, patiently you will see them. When they come in the winter, they travel in the foggy snow, and when they come it 's hard to explain the peace that comes with the warmth of the misty snow.

They come together to find us at those moments when we are feeling most lonely, as a reminder that we are never alone. They come to stay and sit with us for awhile until we are at peace again, and with them, come the stories that heal us.

With each visit comes another thought, another feeling, another message not to be forgotten. The most powerful message being, we are never alone and all our relations that have gone before us, are always with us.

This book came to a close during the last of winter's snow. The final chapter of this book was completed during the anniversary time of when my sister lost her battle with mental and emotional illness so many years ago.

Much like my uncle, at the very worst of these moments, my sister would refuse to speak to me, deny our sisterhood, and order me to leave. I never left. As with my father's example, it never occurred to me to not fight to hold on to my sister and my best friend, for they were one in the same.

By the time that her body was found, she had already closed her eyes and crossed over into the spirit world, long before her time. For eighteen years my sister and I slept side by side, each morning I would wake to the feeling of her eye lashes on my cheek, we called them butterfly kisses. Imprinted on my mind-body-heart and spirit is the moment that I knew my sister's spirit had crossed over.

For unexpectedly I felt a butterfly kiss touch a tear that slid down my cheek and in my heart I knew that the butterfly was gone. The official final word did not come until almost a month later.

For at that very moment, the north wind blew through my heart and spirit and threw me about in such a way that I believed I would never find my balance again. And in the aftermath of trauma, I am reminded that this is an ache that will stay with me for the rest of my days.

My father was right; I already knew that trauma had taken up residence in our family and our hearts once again.

Free Falling

It would be fair to say that from that point on, trauma seemed to be doing more than passing through. Sometimes there are connections between happenings that we cannot see right away and the ties that bind. For several years after losing my sister, my father quite suddenly and unexpectedly closed his eyes and crossed over to the spirit world as well. He didn't even ask if it was okay to do so; he just crossed over.

Just when I thought I had regained my balance from the loss of my sister, trauma grabbed hold of me again. Like many, I thought I was in control and that I had a handle on everything. Why wouldn't I think that?

My spiritual path is a little different then the those of the larger family, so when there was an open casket, I knew that it was best if I did not see my father in this way, so I intentionally made it through the funeral home visiting without one glance in his direction. My last time with my Dad was so warm and vivid in my heart and mind, and this is what I chose to hold on to.

Overall I managed until after everything was finished. After the service I went back to the funeral home with my sister to pick up photos. While I was there, I asked the funeral personnel if I could have one private moment at my father's casket. He came back and told me I could visit with him downstairs and pointed me towards another room that was cold and dark.

For some reason, I thought that my father would still be in the viewing room, where we last saw him. But why would he be? We were all gone, no more visiting, no more words, no more prayers, we were gone and so was he to a room that I never knew existed.

My intentions were misunderstood, I just wanted a quiet moment at the side of my father, but when I entered this cold room, the casket had been opened to where I could see my father's face, the very thing I tried so hard to avoid, I don't remember much from that moment on.

Basically, I remember becoming overwhelmed to find him all alone in a cold dark room, how could this be? I wanted to leave but I could not leave him alone, and I wanted to stay with him, but I could not stay with him because he was already gone. And all I wanted to do was to leave a lily at his side.

The absolute shock of that moment launched me into a continued state of free fall, from which alone, I could not recover. The aftermath of trauma which ensued is very difficult to put into words, but all I can say is that for almost two months I hardly knew where I was or who I was.

It felt as if I was frozen in a surreal dream state where I was trapped inside a circle of confused sorrow and my family was on the outside and no matter how hard I tried, I could not reach them, confusion held sway over me!

On a practical level, of course, there were concrete anchors in my daily life that I desperately tried to hold on to. But the feeling of free falling stayed with me for so long, I feared I would never come back.

Had it not been for my husband, I fear I might not have. For no matter how hard I tried, I could not stop free falling and I could not find my balance. Not alone.

Without question, in the aftermath of trauma for the loss of my father, it was the unfaltering love, devotion and compassion of my husband who held on to me so tightly and never let go, that finally brought me back home, to the place where I found my balance once again.

And I can tell you from my darkest moment and the bottom of my heart I knew that it never occurred to him to let go of me!

What would we do without the people sitting next to us in the Circle of Healing? What would we do without the people who hold on to us and refuse to let go? What would we do without our compassionate loved ones? What would our loved ones do if we let go of them? What would we do? What would we do without the champions of our lost souls? Never let go of your people! Hold on as tight as you can no matter how long it takes!

It is fair to say that trauma has come to stay, a reality that my father tried to prepare me for. Since that time, I have learned to be able to be with the silence.

From my Dad's example, I have learned how to make peace with the aftermath of trauma and find a way to live together with here and there and then and now.

Sadly, these are not the only unexplainable events or the only traumatic stories that could be told, but they are important because they provide both the framework and foundation that explains how it is that trauma has taken up residence here.

Blessed are the compassionate listeners and champions of our hearts ~ hold on and don't let go!

Introduction

The Human Condition

The Human Condition speaks to all that is common in each and every one of us. The Human Condition is all of life's experiences that we share, it is what we all call home.

The Human Condition is about the colors of the rainbow that connect all of us to one another, and that tie us together to this experience called "*life.*" When all is well, the colors of the universal rainbow are vibrant, illuminating, warm and all inclusive.

Then there is that moment that comes, when trauma creeps in and challenges us. Challenges our mind, challenges our body and spirit, challenges our sense of balance and our centeredness is altered, perhaps forever. The rainbow of our life force is weakened as it is not as vibrant anymore. We feel diminished and oftentimes lost. But we are not alone. No one is ever alone.

As members of the Human Condition, we sit side by side in the circle of life. As such, it falls to each of us to step in, to be there for each other and to be willing to shine the light to show that "*hope*" is still here. It is our job to hold a hand, to listen or to hold someone who needs to know that they are not alone.

As lifelong members of the Human Condition we are never alone. In good times or in bad, in strength or in weakness or vulnerability we are never alone. In sadness or despair, in pain or confusion, we are never alone. We all stand together. We all sit side by side in the Circle of Life.

This is what it means to be part of the Human Condition and to sit in the circle of compassionate listeners.

Part One:

TRAUMA

Throughout these pages we hope to capture that moment in time
Between then and now
A realization of where we have been
A moment of acceptance
A willingness to disengage from the past
The courage to move onward
An invitation to sit for a moment
To be able to stay with us
Just for a momen
To be still
To know
To embrace
And then the courage of the warrior heart to let go

Kc carterMartinez, Ed.D.

Trauma

One

TRAUMA

Shattered Spirits

There is the day before the trauma, and then there is the moment of the traumatic event. What happens between these two moments in time, seemingly changes one's life forever, as tomorrow never seems to come.

On a fundamental level, we expect that each day our life will be relatively the same and remain as it has always been and that we will always be safe and out of harm's way. We go through each day with the expectation that whatever may come, will be within our ability to manage it. We hope that if and when something does come our way that it will not disrupt our lives, that it will be brief, and we will be able to handle it quickly and put our life back in balance once more.

In today's world, we continually hear stories about others who have experienced a traumatic event or have experienced personal harm in some way. We know that trauma is a given fact of our lives, and we witness on a daily basis that 'bad things do happen to good people.' We journey through our days, unwavering in our determination to remain hopefully optimistic that the unexpected will not find us.

On a practical level, we understand that there will be times when we will face difficult and challenging times. However, we quietly hope that the most devastating of life's traumatic events will not transpire, and those that we love the most will never be in harm's way. And in the quietest of these moments, we hope that these difficult times will never find 'us.'

What do traumatic incidents look like to us? For the most part, we have a general understanding that traumatic events cause physical, emotional and psychological distress. These are significant events that present in many different forms such as natural disasters, car accidents, sudden community violence, witnessing violence, serious illness or sudden death. Additionally, over the past fifteen years, we have expanded our understanding of traumatic incidents to include terrorist activities and the overwhelming fear and harm that people experience during and after these events.

If we look closely, there is a common denominator throughout these types of traumatic events that allows us to create a mutual understanding of what has happened. In events such as these, we have the advantage of being able to 'visually see' what the actual traumatic event looks like and the aftermath that may follow.

Simply put, even in the most traumatic of events, it is much easier for us to understand that 'which we can actually see.' The ability to visualize what has transpired makes it possible for us to develop an understanding of what has happened and to be able to feel and express sympathy and compassion for those directly affected by the event.

While personal traumas share common characteristics with other forms of traumatic events, these individual incidents possess features that are unique to the trauma of this nature. Unlike other events that are witnessed or viewed by others, personal traumas differ in this regard.

Traumatic events such as rape, sexual assault, emotional abuse and physical assault share a distinctive characteristic; these are traumatic events that happen to 'an individual' in an isolated manner by another person, frequently leaving the traumatized person 'feeling' alone and cut-off from others.

Long after the personal trauma is over, those who have been traumatized in this manner, frequently 'feel' alone and isolated.

Personal Traumatic Incidents

For this reason, these personal traumatic incidents stand apart from the larger family of traumatic events, simply because the person who has experienced the personal traumatic incident is usually the only one that knows the incident has happened and is in the unique position of being the only one who can bear witness to that event.

A personal traumatic event is devastating on many levels when suddenly one day we find ourselves faced with the unimaginable, and the unacceptable. This time, when we hear the story about 'someone' that has been traumatized or has been in harm's way, we struggle to comprehend that this traumatic event has happened to us!

How do traumatic events happen in our lives? They happen like this: one moment we are fine, we are living our lives, and feeling confident that we are safe and secure. The next moment, we find that we are not fine; our lives as we have known them have changed, and as we struggle to understand why, our greatest fear is that we will never be the same again.

Unbeknownst to many, this is the power of a *personal traumatic event* one moment something unexpected happens to us and in the next moment even though the actual event is over, everything seemingly changes in our lives.

For the most part, once we have experienced a traumatic event, we feel as if we are not the same, that we are changed forever. For those who have experienced a personal traumatic event, the reality is that we will never be the same again.

Trauma ~ The Shapeshifter

Trauma is like a shapeshifter, it changes all of the time, and frequently confuses us with its presence; it can be quiet, it can come swiftly, it can come softly, and it can come loudly, and welcome or not, it always comes to stay.

Trauma is the great equalizer. Regardless of our race, religion, ethnic background, sexual orientation, socio-economic status, trauma diminishes each and every one of us to the same level, to a common ground. At this level, there are no differences, no barriers between us, we are all the same.

Ultimately, we are left with the one element that is common to all of us; we are all members of the human condition.

The day before trauma we have a rhythm to our lives, a sense of routine, balance, organization and control. As a culture, we tend to live our lives with the mistaken idea that life follows the direction of the picket fence and that all events that happen in our lives transpire as a sequence of events that makes sense and feels safe to us.

Worldview

We all have our sense of Worldview; it is the invisible blueprint by which we live our lives. Within this view, we have a vision of our plan as to how and when events in our life will unfold and the order in which they will happen. When we are confident that our worldview is strong, our sense of balance and physiological homeostasis is deep-seated.

What do we mean when we say physiological homeostasis? Simply put, when all is well within our lives when we feel centered, and our mind-body and spirit are all in tune, all interconnected we experience a sense of physiological homeostasis, a sense of balance. We seem to think that life travels in the direction of the picket fence, in a straight line and in the order that we have determined. It is not that we are not aware that difficult times and painful loss will happen in our lives, it is just that we tend to assign these events to the furthest points in the sequence of events in our lives so that they happen later in our lives (*with secret hopes that they will never happen*).

As we take the first step in the journey towards healing, we start off alone. The starting point in this journey finds us exactly where we left ourselves, at the moment when the personal traumatic event ended, the place where we are most alone.

The Day Before

For many there is the day before the traumatic event, and then there is the moment of the personal traumatic event. Here is the moment where time stands still for so many; seemingly there is no tomorrow. Afterward, we come to understand that it is this very moment that the hearts~minds~spirits of those who have been traumatized are irretrievably transformed in such a way, that we believe we will never be the same.

To begin this journey towards healing, we need to be willing to step away from the moment of the personal traumatic incident. It does not matter how long ago the traumatic event took place until we understand why we remain at that moment in time; we cannot move away.

When we cling to the trauma of our past, we are focused on what was and on what has already transpired. When our focus remains fixated on wounds of the past, we greatly diminish our ability to understand that there is nothing we can do to change the past; what's done, is done.

By continuing to fixate, we are unable to be present in our daily lives and to move forward to our future. By clinging to past trauma, we guarantee that we will continue to suffer as if it were yesterday. In this way, we continue to leave the door open to our past pain and sorrow and to raise barriers between where we are at this moment in time and our ability to fully be present in our lives.

If we wish to begin the healing journey, it is important to understand that our thoughts shape how we live our lives. Thus, whatever our thoughts tell us about what we are or how we are, is what we believe to be true, resultingly we live our lives in the shadows of these thoughts and judgments.

It is essential to recognize that even in the face of the most horrific of personal traumas, we own the ability to monitor our thoughts and to create a more compassionate understanding regarding how we see ourselves. In the same way, that we would wish to offer compassion and kindness to someone else who has been in harm's way, we need to learn how to do so for ourselves.

When we start off on the journey to healing, we have to make the decision as to how we want to make peace with the traumas of our past. The choice that we make will guide the healing journey that we will take.

How Do You Want to Live

For healing to begin, the question needs to be asked: 'How do you want to live with this personal traumatic experience?' We can consider two possible options from which to respond to this question: we can decide (1) to either live with the trauma or (2) to live through the trauma.

Some might say that there seems to be very little difference between the two, but there is a subtle difference that determines how we will move forward from that moment. In making a decision, we should understand that by choosing to *live with* the trauma, our journey will help us find a way to hush the never-ending noise that we hear in our hearts and minds, so that it is bearable.

If we chose to *live through* the trauma, our journey would help us find a way to hush the noise and to find a way to put these memories in a quiet place as we move beyond them. In the aftermath of a personal traumatic event, this decision is crucial, because it is a reflection of our decision to move forward and an expression of how we wish to live the rest of our lives.

For many, this is a complicated decision as some feel that the traumatic event is a permanent thread in the tapestry of their life and will always remain so. While others perceive the traumatic event as an incident that happened in the past, that it is over, and it will have no bearing on the rest of one's life.

Being able to understand the difference between these two perspectives and the importance of this decision is often the first step in bringing down the barriers between the traumatized and our compassionate listeners. It is also the first step in building the bridge of compassion and understanding between the two.

The journey to healing is a long-lasting one that requires the empathy, kindness, and acceptance of our compassionate listeners. While they may not have been part of the trauma in our past, compassionate listeners and loved ones are irreplaceable in the journey to the future.

It Does Not Matter

It does not matter whether we consider ourselves 'a victim' or a 'compassionate listener.' *Permission Granted* provides the opportunity for all of us to listen to those who wish to give a voice to their story.

Permission Granted invites us to sit side by side in empathetic silence with those who choose to sit in quiet reflection.

In the course of these pages, we are transported from the moment that the traumatic event ends to the moment when the journey to healing is decided upon. For many this is a very powerful moment, for it is the first time since the traumatic incident happened when we realize once more that 'we do' have the power and the right to make our choices.

The first casualty of a personal traumatic event is the loss of the ability to make 'choices'; the ability to choose what will happen or what will not occur. Recapturing the awareness that the ability to 'choose' or to 'decide' is a personal right, is a very empowering moment, perhaps one of the first steps in the healing journey.

Before we move on, let's take a moment to reflect on these four questions:

(1) Are you tired of how you feel on a daily basis?

(2) Do you ever think or feel that you will never be the same again?

(3) Do you ever feel tired trying to manage your thoughts and emotions?

(4) Do you ever wish that tomorrow will be different?

At the end of this reading, our hope is that we are ready for tomorrow.

Native Inspiration

Lakota Instruction for Living

Friends do it this way, that is
Whatever you do in life
Do the very best you can
With both your heart and mind
And if you do it that way
The power of the universe
Will come to your assistance
if your heart and mind are in unity

When one sits in the hoop of the people
One must be responsible
Because all of creation is related
And the hurt of one is the hurt of all
And the honor of one is the honor of all
And whatever we do
effects everything in the universe

If you do it that way, that is
If you truly join your heart and mind as one,
Whatever you ask for
That's the way it is going to be

White Buffalo Calf Woman

Whispers

Grief on Fire

No one tells us about
This thing called grief
No one tells us about
Sorrow's burning embers
That engulf our wounded heart

No one tells us...
There is no remedy
To ease the burning heart

No one tells us...
Only time will ease
Our tarnished souls

Only time...
Will ease our aching hearts

Kc carterMartinez, Ed.D.

Personal Notes:

Chaos

Two

The Aftermath of Trauma

A Quiet Read

This book is meant to be a simple, quiet read to help us understand what it means to live in the aftermath of a traumatic event and to enhance our understanding of what it means to live with the sorrow of personal trauma. We hope to understand *why* we seem unable to leave the past behind and why we cannot find our way to tomorrow.

This quiet reading is intended to help us understand why our inability to speak is so often misunderstood as 'our refusal' to speak.

It is also meant to help those who are nontraumatized who frequently misunderstand the experience of personal traumas, by basing their perception of what it means to be traumatized on one's willingness to verbalize the details of such an event.

After the shock of trauma, the world seemingly becomes divided into two different groups: 'those who know' what it means to be traumatized and 'those who do not know.' The presumption is that if you have never experienced a personal traumatic event, then you cannot possibly understand how it feels to have been traumatized.

This point of view limits our potential for healing, for no one can heal alone for it is the support, acceptance, and understanding of others that encourage and enable us to begin the healing journey.

Traumatic events of any nature are disturbing, but personal traumatic events are outside of the range of ordinary human experience. The impact of these events is distressing to both the traumatized and nontrauamatized.

Creating Barriers

One should never start the journey to healing alone, for it is a journey that requires both solitude and companionship and not just from those who share the experience of trauma. When we separate others into only two possible groups, we are creating barriers to our healing and recovery. When we rule people out as possible resources or simply as an understanding person, we limit access to others who may be willing and able to help us.

When we start to label others, it is the equivalent of assigning people to separate silos: (1) those who have the ability to understand and (2) those who do not have the ability to understand the experience of trauma.

Silo-centric thinking is counter productive as we are only able to see and understand the perspective and experience contained in that unique environment. Under these conditions, we are unable to access or benefit from the understanding, compassion, and kindness of those who we assign to the other silo, which we understand as being 'different' from our own.

Silo-centric thinking only serves to reinforce barriers between people, to keep people separated and diminish the opportunity to sit together in a circle of compassionate silence. In the early aftermath of a traumatic event, 'words' are not always available or necessary, but compassionate, supportive silence is always welcome.

We hope to break down the barriers that exist between the traumatized and non-traumatized, and to build a bridge of understanding that enables everyone to sit together in the circle of compassionate listeners, where there are no expectations, only acceptance and a willingness to be supportive and listen.

When our 'worldview' is compromised, we lose our sense of balance and centeredness, our physiological homeostasis is challenged which creates a fear-provoking awareness of the overall meaning of the loss of control that we feel.

Free Falling

We experience this loss of control and balance in our lives as an overwhelming sense of *free falling*,' a condition wherein we are unable to reestablish our sense of balance, and under these circumstances, chaos ensues.

Within this experience, it is common to feel a sense of alienation or disconnect from ourselves and all aspects of our personal lives. Under these circumstances, chaos has the unusual ability to generate conditions that ultimately create the perfect emotional storm from which we feel there is no escape.

The prism from which we view our 'worldview' is primarily responsible for our deep-seated belief that 'we are' in control of our lives no matter what may come.

The loss of this conviction combined with the experience of 'free falling' makes it almost impossible to re-establish our sense of balance, control, and physiologic homeostasis. The difference between 'worldview' and 'chaos' is fear-provoking, and the experience is overwhelming.

In many ways, we feel evicted from our lives, and become consumed by the notion or fear that we will never be able to regain that control again.

Trapped in the continued state of free-falling we find ourselves wavering between the loss of everything that we have known about our lives and the ever growing fear of the unknown. Our greatest fear being that we will never be the same again.

Recovery and healing are about finding a way to bridge the gap between the moment of the actual traumatic event and our current lives. It is about understanding the importance of being able to close the door on the past traumatic event and the willingness to explore the 'afterwards' of a traumatic event.

To that end, the ability to be able to understand the difference between 'traumatic events' and 'trauma' is crucial to being able to choose the path to healing, this is perhaps the key that opens the door to both understanding and acceptance.

It is not unusual to find that many people are unaware that there is a difference between a 'traumatic event' and 'trauma.' However, for those who have been traumatized, the ability to distinguish between the two is largely important in being able to move forward in one's healing and recovery. At the same, it is equally important for the nontraumatized to be able to understand the difference between the two, for this understanding will allow us to sit in the circle of compassionate listeners and offer support to those in need.

Traumatic Events and Trauma Are Not the Same

A *traumatic* event is an actual incident that occurs when an individual experiences a traumatic injury of some nature. Simply put, a traumatic event is on some level a form of tangible evidence that something outside the range of ordinary human experience has happened, the event itself has a beginning and an end.

Trauma is what comes about after the traumatic event has ended. It is the aftermath of a traumatic event which by its very nature is usually able to be seen, suggesting that there is some form of visible evidence or recall that an incident has in fact occurred. Trauma, on the other hand, is invisible; it is the remnant or aftermath of the incident which creates a disturbing sense of unrest that affects the mind~body and spirit. Since it reflects 'what we cannot see' it is almost impossible to put into words.

How then do we express the overwhelming horror of our experience? To a large extent we enter into a period where we do not even attempt to do so. Trauma is so overwhelming and all-consuming that we find ourselves in a frightening state of relentless confusion.

The same five stages of grief and loss that apply when we lose a loved one are also useful when recovering from a traumatic event: denial, anger, bargaining, depression, and acceptance.

In the aftermath of a traumatic event, we experience a myriad of different cognitive and emotional stages as we attempt to process what has happened. Since personal traumas are so complicated, it lends itself to an additional stage of processing that manifests almost immediately.

It is not unusual for the behaviors or actions of someone who has experienced a personal traumatic event to be perceived as experiencing the early stages of denial in the grief process. When a traumatized person cannot give voice to what has happened to them, they are usually described as being in denial.

In many ways, this explanation does seem reasonable, but when it comes to the complexities of 'personal traumatic events,' there is another possibility that we should consider.

Disbelief vs. Denial

Denial implies a refusal or inability to acknowledge or accept what has happened. However, in personal traumatic events, there is another possible explanation that is a component of the state of free falling that we talked about earlier. While in this state of free falling many victims of personal incidents are quite naturally in a state of *disbelief* which is very different from denial.

When an event is so awful that one is pushed beyond the limits of understanding, one remains in a state of disbelief, simply 'unable' to process what has happened and to absorb the impact of this event. In a continued state of 'disbelief,'one is neither here or there.

In our efforts to bridge the gap between the traumatized and the nontraumatized, we hope to bring empathy and understanding to both. As painful as it is for the traumatized to live with this struggle, it is equally as difficult for concerned friends and loved ones to bear witness to the pain and sorrow of their loved ones.

By bridging the gap between the two, *Permission Granted* extends an invitation to all, simply as members of the human condition to come and sit together in the cirlce of compassionate healing.

Native Inspiration

May the stars carry your sadness away
May the flowers fill your heart with beauty
May hope forever wipe away your tears
May silence make you strong

Chief Dan George

Silence

寂静

Three

There Are No Words

I Cannot Tell You

When it comes to trauma, 'silence' is greatly misunderstood by both the traumatized and the nontraumatized. In the aftermath of a personal traumatic event, one of the first things that another person will ask is 'what happened' or they will say 'tell me what happened.' The meaning and importance of these words differ, depending on who is asking the question.

If the person asking the question is a 'concerned friend or loved one' the question comes from a place of concern and need to understand. If the individual asking the question is a person in a professional role, the questions are necessary for them to be able to determine how to help, as uncomfortable as the questions may be, they are necessary for others to help us at a very sensitive and challenging time.

For the moment, let's step away from the framework of a personal traumatic event and change the frame. Let's change the situation to a traumatic event that we all can easily imagine and understand.

Many of us have been in some form of a car accident

ourselves, or someone we care about has been in an accident. When 'we' have been in an accident, we are initially overwhelmed with intense, confusing feelings about what has happened. At first, if possible, we try to take a quick physical inventory to determine 'if' we are physically 'OK' or if we are hurt in any way.

First responders who take action in response to car accidents and prioritize our needs will (1) Determine safety risks, (2) Determine our physical condition and (3) Then our 'emotional' state before asking any other questions. After establishing our physical safety and needs, they might then ask (4) Is there someone you would like us to call? We understand the rationale behind these questions is because the answers will help to determine how best to assist us at that moment in time.

Questions

We know that the first responders are there to help and one of the most significant rescue tools they have 'to help us' are questions. Questions, produce answers and answers provide information that contributes to guiding decisions as to what we might need at that point.

If you have ever received a call that someone you love has been in a car accident, we all know how frightening that can be. We automatically shift into 'high alert' we have answers to our questions. The first question we might ask is 'how bad is it?' The second question we might ask is 'Are they ok?' And in the absence of actually being able to see that scene of the accident, whether we say it or not, quite often we wonder 'Are they alive?'

We understand the reason we need to ask these questions is in the absence of being able to be at the scene of the accident, we are not able to actually 'see' what has happened. In a sense, we are in a state of emotional limbo because we cannot see our loved one at that moment and are unable to see how they are. We are in the land of the unknown, which is very frightening when it comes to traumatic events and those that we love.

Answers

We need answers to (1) understand what has happened, (2) confirm that they are ok and (3) to know what 'we' need to do at that point. Unless we ask these questions, we will not know or understand what has happened to those that we love or how we can help.

We all understand that these reactions and series of questions in response to a car accident are quite reasonable.

Generally speaking, we expect that first responders 'will' ask us questions to (1) understand what has happened and (2) understand the current condition we are in and (3) what is the appropriate level of care we need at that time.

Because personal traumatic events are only 'visible' to the person who has experienced the traumatic incident, the details, impact and the aftermath of such events often remain 'invisible' to the outside world. Unlike a car accident, where there is visible physical evidence that 'something has happened', personal traumatic events remain invisible in the minds of others who were not involved.

As we mentioned earlier, while personal traumatic events are very similar to other traumatic incidents, the 'invisible' nature of these assaults, sets them apart from the larger family of traumatic events. More often than not, people who have suffered from this form of traumatic events are unable to respond to questions or process responses in the same way as others who have experienced 'other' forms of a traumatic incident.

We might wonder why this is; the answer is simple, personal traumatic events are very different simply by the virtue of the fact that these incidents are both 'deeply personal' and 'invisible'. The 'invisible' attribute is what affects when and how questions can be presented and if they can be answered.

What Happened?

Strange as it seems, the responses to the following two questions are often baffling to both the traumatized and nontraumatized: (1) What happened?: The answer is very often 'I don't know what happened' or (2) Can you tell me what happened?: The answer is very often 'I can't tell you what happened.'

Herein lies the paralyzing power of disbelief and sorrow as it is so inescapable, we are simply unable to speak or to give a voice to the grief and disbelief of our broken hearts. To protect ourselves, we seek shelter in the sanctuary that silence offers us.

This voice of doubt and disbelief resonates throughout our mind-body- spirit; *'If you did not see what happened to me, how can you believe what happened to me? I cannot tell you.'*

The Chameleon

If trauma is like a shapeshifter, then silence is like the Chameleon, possessing an elusive ability to protect itself. The Chameleon cloaks itself in silence and blends into the environment, in this way it remains protected and invisible to others.

At the same time, the Chameleon possesses the unique ability to be able to 'blend in unseen' and the capability to be able to 'see others' while remaining protected and invisible.

Then again, the ability to change colors reflects an additional capacity in the Chameleon's world because the Chameleon can change its color to reflect its emotions and moods. The ability of the Chameleon to camouflage or change mirrors the complexities of 'silence' as it is so often misjudged to have only one meaning or appearance.

In many ways, we should take great comfort in knowing that Mother Earth has provided us with examples from the animal world which are part of our physical world. Through these examples, we begin to understand how they use their ability to change or shift in the face of crisis, stress or fear until they feel safe enough to be visible to others. These examples should help us to begin to understand the intricacies of trauma and its relationship to silence and our ability to change as we start the healing process.

So often our failure to understand the complexities of 'silence' are restricted to a solitary perception, that our silence or our inability to speak means we are intentionally choosing not to speak. Nothing could be further from the truth, yet too often both the traumatized and nontraumatized adhere to this simplistic thinking as if it were the only possibility.

Emotional Wounds

When we think of chaos, there is a sense of crazy- making where we are surrounded by confusion and a deep sense of uncertainty. Peace and tranquility do not live here. And yet, if one is a victim of a personal traumatic event, the silence that one carries within this chaos is deafening, and we are the only ones that can hear it.

The aftermath of trauma creates a widespread silence that infiltrates every aspect of our lives. But it is not a comfortable silence because it is not silence by choice.

The impact of trauma is experienced throughout our physiological, emotional and spiritual experience because it is not possible for trauma to affect only 'one part of us', we are affected as a whole.

The emotional wounds of personal trauma silently imprint on our mind-body and spirit, and how that looks and what that feels like is different for every person. Even as we travel the healing journey, we come to understand that these imprints will be with us forever, but it is up to us how we will live with them.

Unfortunately, the culture that we live in has a limited understanding of trauma and silence that resonates something like this: *"The personal traumatic injury happened if you can 'tell me' what happened.' And "If you cannot tell me what happened, then maybe It didn't happen.'*

These types of social constructs support the argument culture that has become so familiar to us in the course of our daily lives. We are so busy being confrontational that we polarize each other at every turn. When it comes to understanding personal traumatic incidents, polarization only serves to separate us even more and further the divide between the traumatized and nontraumatized.

Why Would Anyone?

In such a contentious culture we cannot tolerate 'silence' as it makes us very uncomfortable. As a result, we have come to the point where we validate someone else's experience by how much they will tell us, how much they will verbalize. At the same time, we have our limitations as to just how much we can listen when someone is trying to tell us of harm that has come to them.

Our culture greatly misunderstands the deep-rooted relationship between traumatic events and silence, as well as the power of both the 'spoken' word and 'the unspoken word.' In a world where 'silence' is stigmatized it is beyond the grasp of many, to understand that 'silence' has a sound and power of its own.

Because we think that this perspective is the only way of understanding silence, we use this refrain to validate or invalidate the trauma and harm experienced by others.

We have to think then, why would anyone want to 'talk about' what has happened under these circumstances? Why would anyone wish to share with others what they have experienced?

We need to ask ourselves if this were 'me,' would I want to break my silence and tell anyone about this? And then we might find ourselves thinking, there has got to be a better way!

The answer is, 'yes' there is another way. Long before there were talk therapies and counseling there were spiritual and community practices strongly based on respecting silence. The answer is, 'yes' there is another way.

Different spiritual paths practice rituals that involve the community working together to help a member in distress. For many, 'silence 'is the expected norm.

Spiritual Paths

Both Buddhist and Native American practice have a strong non-verbal orientation in that they prefer to listen more than they do to speak. In Native communities talking just to talk or to hear your voice is frowned upon, as small talk and idle gossip are not valued. Within these circles, it is believed that words carry power within them, and when spoken are more powerful than the written word.

Core cultural values in the Native world recognize and re- spect the individual and only verbalize thoughts and opinions when asked. In this way, 'thought' comes before the speech and much time is given to thinking before speaking. In both the Native and Buddhist traditions 'quietness' or 'silence' not only contribute to healing from unfathomable situations but is also necessary.

Here in these communities, silence is respected, consid- ered to be powerful and is at the heart of healing. To a certain extent, silence protects us from what we are not ready to know. In the face of all that we have lost, it protects what little pride and dignity we have left.

Never surrender your dignity in response to a personal traumatic event, it belongs to you and it cannot be taken from you. Even if for a time, words fail you, seek refuge in silence where you can hold tight to your dignity and regain your strength.

So often in the aftermath of trauma, we mistakenly think that 'we' decide if we are going to speak. On some level, we believe that we have the ability to decide when we will speak and what we will say. In the face of others demanding verbal proof and disclosure of personal traumatic incidents, we discover that this is not possible.

Basically, we are simply unable to speak or to give a voice to our emotional and spiritual devastation. Unbeknownst to many who struggle with the aftermath of trauma, there are some valid physiological reasons for this that we simply do not have any control over. Our ability to speak in the aftermath of trauma is greatly controlled by our biological and physiological responses to trauma.

Given enough time, patience and compassion, we will come to understand that 'questions' are a rescue tool that is intended to help us. The moment will come, when we will be able to sit still long enough to listen quietly to the questions. Each of us will find the moment when we are ready to give a voice to our pain and sorrow.

Until that time, we remain sheltered in the sanctuary that silence provides for us. For too long, so many have been waiting for 'Permission' to speak. We are here to say *Permission Granted* whatever you chose to say or how you decide to tell your story.

Part Two

CHOICES

Voices

Let's talk about this thing called 'trauma'~
Have I told you that I am always afraid?
There is no devastation like that to the soul
And you thought that I didn't know
That you were still here?

All the talk has been about what
'You took away from me' ...
How you evicted me from my life
At that moment,
They call 'the dark night of the soul'...
But no one ever talks about
Everything you left with me ~
So let's talk about that!

A curse to always be fearful
The burden to always be afraid
Like an albatross around the neck
Your memory hides within the shadows of my mind

Never leaving me alone
You can't patch it - you can't mend it
At least, that's what I am told ...

But I want you to know ...
I know that you are here ...
I am aware that you have taken up residence...
Here in the shadows of my mind

But not today - today I take a stand...
Consider this moment your eviction notice
Guess what? - You can't live here anymore

I am evicting you from the shadows of my memories
They belong to me and me alone
I am here to tell you
That this is not your life - it is mine-
And guess what?
YOU don't live here anymore

Kc carterMartinez, Ed.D.

Native Inspiration

Silence is the mother of truth.

Chief Luther Standing Bear
Teton Sioux

Choices

Four

QUIET SILENCE

Words

Nontraumatized words both silent and spoken take on a life of their own because they express the heartbreak of our broken spirit and wounded heart. Silent words resonate throughout the heart-mind and spirit of the wounded, as even words which we are unable to speak possess a power that only the wounded can hear within.

The great mystery of personal trauma is the role that silence has in protecting us from realities that we are not yet ready to acknowledge. At the same time, while silence protects us in the early aftermath of trauma, it is also an essential factor in helping us to move forward in the process of healing.

In basic terms, without the sanctuary that silence affords us immediately after a traumatic event, we would just fall apart. The longer we live with the horror of our pain in isolation from others, silence finds a way to encourage us to find a way to sit and listen to our stories. When it comes to the telling of our stories, our voice is the first voice that we hear when we wish to walk out of the darkness.

When we look further than ourselves and the community that we live in, we find that other cultures and spiritual pathways have traditional practices and rituals that are part of their healing process that does not demand or call for an immediate use of words. In fact, quiet silence is the accepted norm of those who are struggling with an emotional storm. Compassionate listeners of these communities believe that it is both the silent support and voice of the community members that protect those that are wounded.

Within both Buddhist and Native cultures, silence is greatly respected. In this way, great thought comes before speech, and at the same time the right of the wounded to remain silent until they have had time to explore their thoughts and feelings is honored.

Silence is both respected and expected in times of great emotional turmoil or confusion. By sitting side by side in the healing circle, we show respect to others by not speaking before being asked to speak and by carefully choosing our words.

Moreover, Buddhist and Native communities recognize the value and importance of 'quietness' as the place to be when faced with uncomfortable conditions, for in 'quietness' one can remain silent. As with silence, 'quiet' is understood to play a part in the healing process. It is within this peaceful silence that we begin to explore the story of our traumatic incident.

In time, we come to understand that we are not as helpless as we have been left to feel and that we have the ability to make choices about who we are and what we want to be.

A Victim *or* A Victim *of or* None of the above

Trauma involves sitting with and living with suffering, yet the responsibility for healing is ours and ours alone. In the course of this time of silence, we may find ourselves feeling victimized and helpless. It falls to us to be vigilant not to permit the aftermath of personal trauma to hold us as emotional hostage's nor to allow it to hold sway over our lives.

We have the power to make choices and the strength and courage to avoid the danger of thinking of ourselves as victims. Once we fall prey to this manner of thinking, then that is what we will become; we are what we believe we are. It takes all the energy we can muster up to prevent ourselves from becoming captive to the feelings, thoughts and emotions that connect us to personal traumatic incidents.

Choices

The journey to healing invites us to make many choices, and one of the most important decisions is in respect to how we see ourselves. We should remember that we begin the journey to healing when we make our first choice: (1) to *live with* our trauma or (2) to *live through* our trauma.

The second choice we need to make is in respect to how we see ourselves in the aftermath of a traumatic incident. As there are possibilities to choose from, the choices we make are crucial as to how we will see ourselves as we travel the journey of healing.

The second casualty in the aftermath of a personal traumatic event, is we lose our sense of 'self', of who we are. As time goes on, we have an persistent need to explain our experience and to define how we see ourselves now, in the aftermath of trauma.

While these choices may seem inconsequential, it is essential that we understand how important it is to think carefully about the choices that we make. Our choices define our mindset and how we will see ourselves and understand our experience as we move forward. All of our decisions should be based on the *intention* not to permit the traumatic events that we have suffered to define the rest of our lives.

When it comes to rape and sexual assault or any form of assault, there is a driving need to frame the experience in a way that 'explains what happened to us' and what that experience means to us now.

As such, we have some options to consider; with the first choice, there is the option to explain our experience by saying that we are 'a Rape victim' or a 'Sexual Assault victim' or an 'Assault victim.'

If we choose this explanation, we continue to live as if the event is ongoing, almost like an instant replay. This type of thinking causes us to feel that the traumatic event is going on and on and that we can never escape it.

By embracing this perspective, we guarantee that we will continue to suffer, even though the traumatic event is long over. It ensures that we will never be able to live fully in the present moment of our daily lives.

As an alternative possibility, we have the option to explain our experence as 'A victim *of* rape' or 'A victim *of* sexual assault.' The key phrase in this choice is 'A victim of' as this perspective strongly infers that the personal traumatic event that we have experienced is something that happened in the past and is now over.

The difference between these two interpretations is that the phrase 'Rape victim' conveys a label mentality that we will carry with us wherever we go. Too often people who chose to see themselves as 'Rape victims' or 'Sexual Assault victims' or victims of any form of assault encircle themselves in a cloak of victimhood that seems to follow them wherever they go regardless of how long ago the personal traumatic event occurred.

In contrast, the phrase '*A victim of*' advocates for an explanation of a personal traumatic event that happened in the past that is acknowledged, yet remains just that, an interpretation of a past event and not a life sentence to victimhood.

There was a time when it seemed that there were limited possible explanations or choices to make in an effort to explain one's experience. Yet recently it seems that there have been some changes in the collective social mentality on personal traumatic events, and another alternative has surfaced.

None of the Above

For many years, conversations seemed to focus on the notion that options were narrow when attempting to define one's experience and one's definition of 'self' post the traumatic event. More recently, though, another voice has been added to the conversation that considers choices. Let's call this voice: *None of the above.*

Across time and conversations, many women have rejected the concept of 'victim' at any level as they vehemently reject this social notion that can be summed up in the following accounts: 'Do not call me a victim. 'Do not call me a survivor.' 'Don't pigeonhole me, it doesn't work for me.' *And:* 'I am none of these labels' or 'I have control over my life, and I make my decisions about my future.' *As well as:* 'If I have to define myself, then just call me a fighter' or 'I am a woman who experienced trauma, I decide what to do next,' and 'I am responsible for making my choices.' *And finally* 'Don't call me any of those labels, they don't work for me because I decide what happens next.'

In the long run, we have to be able to offer more than just seeing ourselves as a 'victim' with a lifelong membership to the sisterhood of victimization.

These are very personal choices. No one can make them for us; however, to begin the journey to healing; it is necessary that we make these two decisions.

On the actual traumatic event: (1) We are choosing to *live with* the traumatic event, or (2) We are choosing to *live through* the traumatic event.

Secondly, to find a way to define our experience of the traumatic event: (1) As a rape victim or (2) As a victim of or (3) As 'None of the above.' The decisions we make are crucial to how we see ourselves in the aftermath of a personal traumatic event.

If we always choose to see ourselves as just a 'victim,' then that is what we will become. In this way, it will not matter how long ago the personal traumatic event happened, as it will seem as if it is always yesterday. This perspective challenges our ability to live a full, present, healthy and balanced life.

While these two steps might seem slight and perhaps insignificant, it is essential that we realize how important they are to our present life and our future ability to heal and to live a fully present life.

At the end of the day, we need to ask ourselves: 'Who do I want to be?' 'How do I want to see myself?' 'How do I want others to see me?' 'How do I want others to understand my experience?' The choices that we make will have a direct impact on the responses to these questions.

Healing work is very painful work; there is no way to escape this reality. But to begin the healing journey, we need to start to understand 'where we have been' and 'why' we seem unable to leave that moment in time.

Painful work requires great patience with ourselves, and as simple as this may sound; it is very difficult to achieve when we are so confused and at odds with ourselves. We are talking about making some difficult decisions and choices, at a time, when we can barely sit still or connect one thought to the other.

In the world of the nontraumatized making decisions or choices is an ordinary course of events througout the day, but not for the traumatized because in the aftermath of trauma we feel evicted from our lives and alienated from our thoughts, feelings, and emotions. In this early stage of trauma, we live a very surreal existence, where others may look at us and think that we are fully functioning and doing just fine, but we know that we are not.

If we were to stand in front of a mirror with a friend or family member and ask them to describe how our reflection looks to them in the mirror, their vision would be dramatically different than what we see. The chaos, pain, anger, and confusion we feel would be reflected in the image that 'we see', but because we are unable to verbalize the traumatic experience, and what we are feeling, others only know what we want them to see.

If we think about it, it is amazing how quickly we become adept at concealing what has happened and how we are truly feeling.

It requires great patience with ourselves to get to a point, where we can calm ourselves long enough to sit and reflect on these questions, on the decisions and choices that we want to make. At the same time, we need to be patient with our loved ones who in time may become our compassionate listeners, because initially our struggle may be difficult for them to understand and to process.

Since all personal traumatic events are not the same, each traumatized person experiences the traumatic event in a different way. Since traumatic experiences differ, so does the telling or sharing of experiences differ, as does the telling or sharing of the trauma to others. The longer we go on 'acting as if we are ok' to those that care about us, the more patience we will need to have with them when the time is ready for us to share our struggle.

Trauma requires patience on all levels with both the traumatized and the nontraumatized. But with patience comes both the ability to listen and the ability to speak, both are our companions as we begin the journey to healing.

Kathleen carterMartinez, Ed.D.

Native Inspiration

Go forward with courage

When you are in doubt, be still and wait
And when doubt no longer exists for you
Then go forward with courage
So long as mists envelope you, be still
Be still until the sunlight pours through and dispels the mist,
As it surely will
Then act with courage

Ponca Chief

Whispers

If all you can do

If all you can do Is cry
Then cry...

If all you can do is wait
Then wait...

If all you can do is weep
Then weep...

But remember...

I am here for you
And when the healing journey
Calls you home...
I will take that journey with you...
You are not alone.

Kc carterMartinez, Ed.D.

Tears

Five

EMOTIONAL STORM

Acting As If

So often the image that we see in the mirror is profoundly different then the likeness that others see when they look at us. To some extent, the appearance that others see reflects the illusion of our physical/emotional and mental condition that we want them to see.

Generally speaking, we are all capable of creating a persona or an image that we wish others to see, even if that persona is not an honest reflection of how we are really feeling.

At the very least, this is a transitional image for the moment, and at best, an elusive facade that hides the crushing loneliness and despair that we feel after experiencing a traumatic event. The image that we project to others is a far cry from the raging emotional storm that we feel within.

Have you had a friend that was always mirror image ready? The kind of person that looks like they have it together at all times? For the most part, the majority of us frequently struggle to look simply like our genuine selves in any reflection. For some of us, the ability to hide or camouflage how we are feeling does not come naturally.

Some people have an uncanny ability to act 'as if' they have no worries, and that all is well, even in the face of the most overwhelming circumstances. Some people are so gifted at acting 'as if' that we might think that they deserve an award for their flawless convincing performance, and yet we often wish that we could do the same.

But what about those of us that struggle with a limited ability to act 'as if' 'and find it difficult to pull off the façade off? And yet, in the aftermath of a traumatic event, we find that even the most amateurish of us possess an incredible ability to appear as if all is well within our world.

The Great Pretender

Enter the great pretender! You know who you are ~ the walking wounded who have perfected the art of pretending not only that all is well but more importantly, perfected the ability to pretend 'as if' nothing has ever happened, 'as if' they have not experienced a personal traumatic event.

This is what it means to act 'as if,' to navigate the day to day appearing as if we are the fully functioning person that others think that we are. We need to understand, that other people perceive us in this way, because of the time and energy we have put into creating the facade that we want them to believe.

In many ways this is our effort to protect ourselves from coming face to face with the aftermath of a traumatic event until we are ready to do so.

Often both the traumatized and nontraumatized are challenged to understand why anyone would want to act 'as if' they are feeling one way when in fact they are feeling another? If you are wounded and hurt, why wouldn't you want others to know? If you are frightened why wouldn't you want others to be able to comfort you?

In the early stages of trauma, the 'Great Pretender' protects us from a devastating experience that we are not yet ready to acknowledge. When experiencing the state of disbelief, we are unsure, of what has happened, yet it is with absolute certainty that we know something has happened.

At the same time, we struggle to accept that we have experienced a devastating personal traumatic event. In this fugue state of confusion and disbelief the *Great Pretender* keeps us mentally, psychologically and spiritually safe, until we are ready to move forward.

During this time, the 'Great Pretender' protects us from harm we are unable to acknowledge and allows us to continue to function in what appears to be a normal way. Anyone who has been wounded in this way understands the pressing need to return to a state of normalcy, to be able to step back into that life which we define as our norm. In many ways, we feel an internal drive to hit the re-set button to reestablish our sense of physiological homeostasis: we have an overwhelming need to reestablish our sense of being in balance once again.

In the same way, that we understand the subtle difference between denial and disbelief, we are called upon to recognize the unique purpose of the 'Great Pretender.' Some misunderstand the appearance of pretending as not being honest, but this could not be further from the truth. In the aftermath of trauma, honesty is frequently equated with the ability or limited ability to discuss one's traumatic experience.

So often when given the opportunity, we will share with you what we can, yet our inability to share with you what we cannot face our self is misconstrued as secrecy or dishonesty, neither one of which have any place in the reality of the aftermath of trauma.

Emotional Storm
(We are not alone; we just think we are)
    At the time of the traumatic event, the emotional wounds of personal trauma silently imprint on our mind-body and spirit

and stay with us, long after the event is over. Each part of our experience is interconnected, so what affects one part of us, affects all of us. These imprints are expressed in the emotional storm that we find ourselves in the midst of in the aftermath of trauma.

As we are caught up in this emotional storm where the winds of anger, disbelief, sorrow and despair toss us around, we find ourselves helpless to quiet the thoughts that haunt our minds or calm the winds that toss us about.

The longer we are caught up in this emotional storm, the more isolated we become, and the lonelier we feel. In our isolation, we convince ourselves that no one else knows that we are struggling and that even if they did, they would not understand our emotional pain and sorrow.

Once we become convinced of something, it is very difficult to change our mind or our perceptions. Loneliness hurts, but left alone for too long; loneliness can distort our thinking and our perceptions, to the point where we convince ourselves that those we hold dearest, are the very ones that we cannot turn to. Within this isolation, we decide what others think and what they will believe before we have even whispered one word.

It is very difficult to be the friend or loved one of someone who has suffered a personal traumatic event. As the wounded, we convince ourselves that those closest to us are unaware that some harm has come to us because we have not told them. But this is an illusion that we create in our isolation, and the longer we stay trapped within this emotional storm, the stronger these thoughts become, eventually becoming our beliefs.

It is not easy to be the friend or loved one of the wounded, because our illusion is not their illusion. Just because we have not given words to our trauma or acknowledged our pain, does not mean that our compassionate loved ones cannot sense that something is terribly wrong.

Friends and Loved Ones (Listen)

As a friend or loved one we perceive many indicators and signs that something is terribly wrong. Even though you have not confided in us that something has happened, we can see that you are not the same. It has not escaped our awareness that you are trying very hard to act 'as if' you are okay and that you desperately want to believe that you are.

But as a friend or loved one, we too can feel when something has changed, when you are not the same, despite the continued effort you exert to create the illusion that you are. Spoken or not, we sense the burden of your pain and struggle to reach out to you.

In the same way, that you fear to acknowledge your experience, we are concerned that you will not find that voice. We fear that you may fade away from us in front of our very eyes, and we will never get you back. Can you imagine the heartbreak of watching someone you care for dearly quietly drift away and fear that while they are standing right there in front of you, you may lose them forever?

Did you know that as your friend or loved one, we too have fears for what we sense, what we see and what we do not understand? Did you know that we are right here in the middle of this storm with you, but you can not see us, you cannot hear us? Did you know that we too are heartbroken and cannot bear the sorrow to see you in so much pain, if only you would let us in? Did you know?

This is what it means to be engulfed in an emotional storm, to feel as if we are alone, when we are not. To feel isolated while at the same time our friends and loved ones are standing right there on the other side of the storm waiting to reach out to us, and we cannot even say *hold on to me!*

This is what it means to be rendered emotionally disadvantaged where we feel so isolated and alone that we cannot reach out to those that we need the most and cannot find our voice to simply say, 'I have been hurt, and I am afraid.' This is what it means to live in the aftermath of trauma and all the fear, pain and sorrow that it entails.

Through the quiet reading of these pages, we hope to build a bridge that connects us one to the other. Regardless of whether we call ourselves 'wounded' or 'friend or loved one.' We are committed to crossing this bridge together, hand in hand as we come together to sit in the circle of compassionate healing.

Native Inspiration

Can we talk of integration of heart and minds?
Unless you have this
You have only a physical presence
And the walls between us
Are as high as the mountain range

Chief Dan George

Sorrow

Six

Footprints In The Clouds

Imprints

As we begin to move forward, we hope that we will not be swayed into going backward. The strength and courage that it takes once the choice is made to go beyond our traumatic event and to begin to move on are considerable. Anyone who has dwelled within the silence of trauma understands how easy it seems to simply stay put and to remain entrenched with the suffering of our past.

Why is this? Because on some level, it almost seems easier to continue to suffer from the pain and sorrow that we live with, rather then begin to focus our energy in a more positive direction on trying to understand 'why' we struggle so.

Once we have an awareness that we are suffering, then we might have to consider doing something about it. And doing something different is often very frightening, as it almost feels as if we are a stranger traveling in a foreign land, but the only thing is, this strange land is our life.

As we begin to move forward, we need to take a moment to reflect on some of the physiological aspects of the traumatic experience. When given the chance to take a physiology course, most of us would pass on the opportunity, because we have a reluctance to understand that the experiences in our lives have a very real physiological basis.

For some reason, we are more comfortable saying, let's skip that chapter and go on to the next, just because it seems a little more complicated than we wish to explore.

To take that first step away from our suffering, we do need to take a moment so that we can develop a basic understanding (1) that we do have a physiological response to traumatic events and (2) of how this reaction may be experienced. Without this basic understanding, we are setting ourselves up to fall backward into our old thinking and behaviors.

To move forward, we need to have an understanding of how the brain affects the balance of the mind-body-spirit. Otherwise, we might not be able to understand some of the feelings, thoughts, reactions that we might experience as we embark on the journey to healing.

In fostering this understanding, we then might be able to answer the question: Why are we stuck at this moment in time? Are there reasons beyond our control that explain why we cannot seem to let go of the past?

Our basic ability to respond, act and speak in the aftermath of a traumatic event and the degree to which we function is significantly influenced by our physiological responses to the traumatic event. Traumatic events impact the balance of our mind-body-spirit experience, as we are unable to separate one from the other.

What happens to one part of our experience eventually filters through to the other areas of the human condition which are all interrelated, and as we know the mind-body-spirit are all interconnected.

So it makes sense that when one part of our human condition experience is affected by a traumatic event, then eventually all of the other components are also affected.

The imprint of trauma on the balance of our overall experience is often invisible. Much the same as we can see footprints in the sand even as the water washes them away, we can visualize the imprint of trauma on our physiological and spiritual experience like footprints in the clouds.

Although we are unable actually to see these footprints, through the imagination of this image, essentially we know that what we sense and feel is somewhere deep within us. Perhaps beyond our vision and perhaps beyond our words, but it is still deep within us.

Wired to Protect

Sometimes we do not understand the relationship between what happens to us physically and emotionally and our brain, and yet this connection has such a profound impact on what we can do and on what we are unable to do.

From the Buddhist point of view, emotions are considered to be destructive if they disrupt our sense of balance or disturb our sense of reality. All of the emotions and elements of a traumatic experience are powerful, disturbing and disruptive.

Whether it is the actual physical harm that is suffered, or the petrifying thoughts that are experienced or the overwhelming, terrifying emotions that are experienced during and after the event. Taken together, all of these experiences greatly disturb our sense of balance, reality, and well-being.

Many if not all of these thoughts and feelings are so overwhelming and unimaginable, that we are simply unable to be consciously aware of these thoughts and feelings or to process them. As such, they remain deeply imprinted within our own internal experience. So how do we handle or manage such overwhelming information?

How could anyone 'take in' such troubling information all at the same time and continue to breathe or to function? What do we do with information that we are not ready to know?

The initial answer is that it is simply not possible, nor is it safe to take all of this information in at the same time, and here is where the amazing functions of the brain come into play. Traumatic events change the way that the brain responds and reacts, in the aftermath of the traumatic event in our everyday lives. What does this mean? It means that what we understand as our 'normal way of being,' our expected way of thinking and responding in our day-to-day lives is now different. It is not the way that we experienced ourselves through the course of our day before the event; it is not how we remember 'being', we feel different.

However, in the early aftermath of trauma, we are not necessarily aware of this shift in the way that our brain responds and reacts throughout our day-to-day interactions. Perhaps we experience nothing more than a subtle awareness that 'we feel different' and the way that we 'think' may in fact also seem different.

Just because we are experiencing suffering, does not necessarily mean that we are fully aware of the source of that pain. In it's role as master of our physiological circuit board, the brain filters the information that our experience brings in, and tries to determine if it is something that we can handle 'knowing' at that given moment.

In the face of the unthinkable where words are not possible, there is a tsunami of incoming information that is very overwhelming and confusing. Almost as a form of executive function, the brain will release or reveal that which we can handle at any given moment.

Our ability to manage information needs to include the entire interconnected mind-body-spirit and not just one aspect of this interdependent system. If all aspects are not fully functioning or capable of absorbing this information, then it will be 'put aside' until sometime in the future when we are in a better safer place to process this information.

Memories and information come to us in different ways, and they are not always in the form of 'data' as some information is simply transient or snippets of memories that might not make much sense to us.

Other forms of perception may be in the form of an 'a sense of' or a tactile sense that 'this moment' feels like a moment in the past that we cannot clearly recall, but the similar circumstances trigger a part of that recall. Even if the mind does not fully remember or cannot fully access that information, the imprint of trauma dwells in the body, and external stimulants can trigger a sensory recall, that is disturbing and uncomfortable in the absence of a history that contains accurate information.

Executive Function

The brain is the gatekeeper to the interdependent mind-body-spirit connection, and it is wired to protect us from what we are not ready to know or experience. In many ways, the brain is the master of the physiological circuit board of our experiences and protector of our feelings, emotions, spiritual and physical well-being.

Our physiological circuit board is very similar to the master circuit board we all have in our home. For the most part, we hardly ever give much thought to it until we accidentally cause an overload and a circuit shuts down within our home. When this happens, we have to go in search of the master circuit breaker box so that we can identify 'which breaker' was overloaded and shut down. Before we can do that, though, we usually need to determine what caused the overload in the system in the first place. Because if we do not and we turn the breaker back on, it will only become overloaded and shut down again, our brain functions very much in the same way.

The brain is one of the largest organs in the body made up of several different lobes and has many different specialized areas that work together towards the overall function of our physiological experience.

To understand how the brain works upon traumatic events, it is helpful to perceive the brain as two halves, the left side, and the right side. Both the left and the right typically work together to help us process our daily experiences, yet their functions are very different. In the ordinary course of the day, the left side of the brain and the right side of the brain work together to organize our experiences in a way that we can understand.

The function of the left side of the brain is to remember facts, the words, the expressions of an event and it can put the experience in order. The right side of the brain, on the other hand, can be described as the 'memory keeper' as it organizes all the other aspects of the same experience such as emotions, sound, and the smell of the experience.

Traumatic events significantly impact both sides of this process which can create a disabling of the functions of both sides of the brain, which is similar to overloading a circuit. Once disabled the left side cannot bring together our experiences in a logically organized manner, they don't make sense the way they once did. If this circuit becomes overloaded, so then does the circuit for the right aspect of the brain.

When we have experienced a traumatic event, the right side of the brain stores elements such as sound, emotions and smells associated with that incident.

Sometimes these senses can be triggered in the present moment 'as if' they are happening again, because the left side of the brain is not fully functioning, the left side helps us to sequence events and keep things in order.

From this perspective, we can see how when balanced both sides of the brain function very well together. But in the aftermath of a traumatic event, our system becomes flooded and overloaded and circuits within our brain shut down in response to an overwhelming horrific event.

As the gatekeeper to our interdependent mind-body-spirit connection, the brain possesses executive functions that have the power to shut down these overloaded circuits until we are in a safer and healthier place to receive and process information that will inform us about the actual traumatic event in a non-threatening manner.

Frozen Brain

From both a clinical and spiritual perspective, this aspect of the traumatic experience is often referred to as 'being frozen', unable to talk, to move or to process. And we can remain in this suspended state for a very long period, until we begin to experience a slight thaw in this frozen condition. At this point we can begin to think just a little bit about what has happened, where we have been and where we are at this moment in time.

This is considered progress, this is considered moving forward when we can start to 'think' about what has happened and to resist the urge to turn away from painful realities.

As we add the elements of the brain and physiology to our expanding understanding of what it means to live in the aftermath of trauma; we should be comforted knowing that so much of how we are, what we do, what we say and how we feel is greatly influenced by our brain and our physiological response to a traumatic event.

It's Not Just Us

At this point, we should breathe a little easier as we begin to understand that to a large extent we do not control our response or reaction to the traumatic event, at least initially. As such, it simply does not come down to our choice, so much of the aftermath of trauma has absolutely nothing to do with our choices, but rather our ability to cope with the aftermath of a horrendous experience, that only time will heal.

This relevant information offers insight for those who struggle with trauma and for the nontraumatized who wish to be of service. As we build bridges of understanding between each other, we begin to take down the walls of 'social misperception' that so often damage our ability to simply to sit side by side to listen to those who wish to use their voice or to offer supportive silence to those who refrain from speaking.

Through sharing information and enriching our insight we significantly improve our ability to simply 'let each other in', regardless of whether we see ourselves as wounded or as compassionate listeners, *perhaps we are both*.

Native Inspiration

Our first teacher is our own heart.

Cheyenne

Part Three

HEALING FROM THE INSIDE OUT

The Teller

Stories and memories
Come from deep within the heart
And mind of 'the teller'...
Each story when told time and time again...
Allows us to reach back
And find our lost selves within our hearts
Even in the most devastating of loses...
Telling has the power to move us away...
From the aching hurt of trauma and loss...
To the healing comfort...
Of the reminders of who we were...
Who we are...
That in time...
Soothes our aching spirit and heart
So says 'The Teller'...

Kc carterMartinez, Ed.D.

Pain

Seven

PAIN AND SORROW

Frozen in Time

When we began this journey, we found ourselves at the very moment that the traumatic event ended and at the moment when the aftermath of trauma began. We found ourselves in a place we never wanted to go, in a place that we never asked to be.

In many ways, without even realizing it, we found ourselves standing on one side of a locked door not understanding how we got there and despite our most courageous efforts, we were unable to open it to come through to the other side. Perhaps we were paralyzed in that very spot, for fear of the unknown of what was on the other side?

We did not know where we were, only that it was somewhere between here and gone, a very frightening place to be. How did we get here? Is there anyone that would come to find us and take us home? Does anyone know that we are lost?

Frozen in time, we remained in that place believing that we would never be able to return from whence we came. Feeling invisible we wondered where everyone had gone, and why were we alone? In isolation, we felt alone and wondered if anyone even knew that we were gone? And even if they did, how could we explain the series of events that brought us to this solitude? How could we tell them where we have been?

But here in this place where we are alone, we have become open-minded and have come to understand that solitude itself is a sacred place; it is the home of inner silence. We cannot live here, but we can stay here for a while because this is where solitude can guide us home to peace, and this is what is needed to begin our journey home.

We begin this journey remembering when we felt helpless as it seemed for all intensive purposes that we would never find our way back home. Yet at this moment, we are preparing to take a step away from our past and to take a step forward to the life that is within our hearts. Was it that long ago that we believed we would never find tomorrow again?

Even in the best of times, there is a tendency to be unaware of the manner in which we are conducting ourselves or of what the patterns of our behavior are.

It is exhausting to live in a way where we are always on guard from others, distant from those around us and very often detached from the present moment. How tiring it must always be to feel that one is neither here nor there? How lost must we feel not to be able to be merely in the only moment that matters, this present moment.

Suffering

It seems to be an inherent part of our human nature to avoid sorrow and problems at all cost. Yet they appear to find us just the same. In many ways, this happens because we do not have a point of reference of what suffering means and what role it plays in our lives or the fact that it plays a central part in our lives.

In the Buddhist way our pain and sorrow are understood as suffering. From this perspective, we are reminded that suffering is a part of life and that there isn't anything we can do to escape it.

Each and every one of us will have our struggles with suffering as it is an intrinsic part of the human condition, for it is an absolute part of our lives and we can not ignore it, nor can we hide from it. The only difference is how suffering will visit our life; as we will all be faced with individual struggles.

Regardless of whether you understand yourself to be traumatized or see yourself as a compassionate listener, suffering belongs to each and every one of us. There is no escaping suffering in this life, there is only acceptance.

The Buddhist perspective encourages us to change the way that we look at suffering and to stop spending so much time and energy trying to avoid them. We need to find a way to see the challenges of suffering in a different light. In what may seem like a confusing teaching, we come to understand that suffering is a part of life and as such, we are challenged to learn how to accept suffering and find a way to cope with it in our lives.

There is a sense of calmness that comes with the initial awareness that we have been living in a certain way, and that we have in fact been experiencing suffering. So often we go day to day without giving much thought to the manner in which we are living our lives. What do we do with our thoughts and feelings? When we are unable to give a voice to our pain, sorrow, and emotions, what do we do with that struggle? How do we handle that suffering?

Buddhism teaches us that the fundamental nature of Buddha Dharma is that suffering is universal to all, common to all of us. In this way, we are all interdependent, all connected, as suffering is an intrinsic part of each of our lives.

Our goal should not be to try to avoid it, because we cannot. Instead, our intention should be to embrace suffering in a positive way and avoid bringing negativity and negative thoughts and emotions into our minds, for if they come into our minds, negativity comes into our lives.

Unlike other cultures and spiritual paths, our culture does not encourage us to acknowledge our pain and suffering, rather that we should avoid it all costs. This form of avoidance comes at a high spiritual cost for each of us as it only creates and contributes to feelings of isolation from each other.

We have the ability to make the decision to do something different and we can choose the path to end what Buddhism understands as our suffering. When we continue to do the same thing, time after time we get the same results, in this way we ensure that our suffering will continue.

How many times do we wake up hoping that these troubling thoughts and feelings are just a bad dream? How often do we go to sleep wishing we did not have these struggles only to wake up to find that they are still with us? How many days do we wake up believing that there is no way out of this vicious cycle of pain and sorrow?

A Cycle Is A Circle

The Buddhist perspective helps us to understand that suffering is central to our lives, but the manner in which we accept and deal with suffering is our individual challenge.

A cycle is a circle, and in many ways the more we hold onto our negative patterns, the more we strengthen that circle. It seems that unknowingly we have confined our suffering to the middle of that circle, and the longer we continue the same pattern of negative thinking, here is where suffering will stay, right smack in the midst of our lives! Maybe we do not understand how it got there, but we certainly have the capacity to change how it impacts our mind-heart and spirit.

The only way we can release our suffering and to find some measure of internal peace is to consciously make the decision to do something different with our pain and sorrow, we can accept it. It is at this moment where the journey to healing begins. It is when we understand that we have the power to transform our pain and sorrow, our personal suffering.

In what might seem like an incomprehensible suggestion, we can learn to make friends with our suffering, we can learn to embrace it. Once we can do so, this will allow us to make room for more positive loving experiences in our life, and we will be able to loosen the hold we have on the circle of our suffering. We can expand the circle of pain to allow others in, to invite them to come and be with us.

Transformation of Suffering

In many ways, it is a relief to be able to say: *I did not know why I was living this way, or I did not know that I was suffering*. There is a tendency for our social norms to encourage us to diminish our pain and suffering to the most marginal of thoughts. In this way, we rarely have the opportunity to embrace the enormousness of our pain and suffering. As a result, we tend to spend a lot of our time pretending that we are not consumed by this suffering.

With awareness comes a subtle sense of tranquility, because we can begin to calm down just enough to allow ourselves to simply sit with our thoughts and feelings. When we suffer we are without inner peace and where there is no inner peace, there can be no outer peace; we are in a state of unrest in both our internal and external worlds. How exhausting is it to be in constant emotional turmoil? Where do we go to find some peace?

There are many Native American spiritual practices that are initiated with the intention of bringing the individual member back into harmony not only with themselves but with their community

Many rituals while symbolic in nature, are often held to bring harmony and healing to a community member in emotional distress and when a member of the circle is in distress, the entire community is affected.

The goal of these rituals is to eventually help the individual reconnect with themselves and ultimately to re-establish harmony within the heart, spirit, and mind of the one who is suffering.

Traditional Native healing practices embrace beliefs that are spiritual in basis and are often used for both emotional and spiritual conditions, from which the individual needs to heal. From the Native perspective, healing is about mending the entire person and not just their emotional struggles, as most illnesses are believed to have their basis in spiritual problems and in spiritual unbalance.

In a sense, from this perspective healing must begin from the inside out as it offers us the understanding that if we are broken in spirit, we are not well, and we are not whole. To heal we need to harmonize our physical, emotional and spiritual aspects and only then will we be in balance again.

Disharmony of Mind and Spirit

Within Native ways, suffering is acknowledged and accepted along with the fundamental belief that suffering results in disharmony of spirit. To regain our balance, healing needs to focus on harmonizing of the spirit. But within this healing practice, the help, support, guidance and silence of others are essential if one wishes to become well.

The underlying message is, we cannot heal alone, we need the help of others around us, and it is the acceptance, strength, support and compassion of others along the journey to healing that will help us the most.

The path to the healing journey begins with learning to live in the present moment. But we cannot do that until we are aware (1) that how we have been functioning in the aftermath of trauma is different than what we consider our normal way of being and (2) that we have been in denial of our pain and suffering. To move forward, we need to learn not to deny our struggle, but simple to change the way that we respond to our thoughts, feelings, and reactions to our past.

Buddhist thought encourages us to develop what is called the internal Dharma, meaning a calm and peaceful mind which will help us in neutralizing the power of the negative mindset. A negative mind creates a disturbed mind which we experience as stressful, and as a feeling of constant unease. Since our social norms discourage us from acknowledging our suffering, we see problems as struggles that we should try to avoid.

However, from both a Buddhist and a Native perspective we are encouraged not to see the troubled mind as a burden, but as an opportunity to transform the pain and sorrow that we are living. Although we are not accustomed to viewing pain, sorrow and suffering in any positive light, we are encouraged to try to recognize the opportunity we are presented with that will allow us to transform our struggles.

The thoughts and memories that arise in the mind cannot be stopped, nor can the emotions that these thoughts evoke. Still, we do not need to remain paralyzed by our suffering. While it may work for for awhile, with awareness we come to understand that we do not have to stay this way, and we can choose an alternative path.

Welcome the Peacemaker

We need to be willing to change if we wish to choose the path of peace, but to do this, takes the courage of the warrior's heart. Both Native and Buddhist pathways inform us that by choosing the path of the peacemaker we can recognize our capacity to embrace the reality of what it means to suffer a personal traumatic event and the change that it brings to our lives. Instead of decrying these changes, we can learn to embrace them.

This speaks to the very core of our suffering, to the internal battle that we have been in the grips of from the moment that the traumatic incident ended. Very simply, this is an internal struggle and one where we are in conflict with ourselves.

To relinquish this conflict, we can choose the path of the peacemaker towards healing.

If we want to stop hurting, we need to stop denying our pain. When we negate our pain a profound sense of heaviness creeps into our minds, and our hearts and when are hearts become heavy we have great difficulty keeping our minds clear and in balance.

Other spiritually minded people have found their way out of suffering and isolation by choosing the path of the peacemaker. At first blush, we might think what does this have to do with us? Peacemakers are needed to settle differences and we might think that we are not at odds with anyone! Yet at this very moment, it seems that perhaps we might be hearing a gnawing quiet whisper that says:

'Yes, you have, you have been at war with yourself
for a very long time, and you know it!'

This is a very profound moment when we can sit still long enough to allow in thoughts that we have been unable to accept. It is also an insightful moment when we embrace the realization that we have been trapped in an ongoing internal battle within ourselves.

The question could be asked why would anyone choose to wage war on themselves? But if you are among the wounded, you know more than anyone else how vehemently we wage this battle within ourselves to avoid accepting the fact that we have been wounded. This battle has been carrying on in the thoughts within our mind and spreads toxic negative emotions throughout our body; this war will not end on its own.

We need to be brave enough to choose the path of the peacemaker because initially we are the only ones that can quiet the emotional storm that rages within us. We have to make a conscious decision to end this battle, to choose the path of the peacemaker, to put our struggles to rest. Before we can listen to the voices of others, we need to be able to listen to our voice. In fact, it will be the very first voice that we can hear.

We all have a deep need to harmonize our deepest feelings and thoughts with our external world; in this way we choose the path of real peace. Both Buddhist and Native spiritual paths encourage us to rebuff the social norms that we are accustomed to with respect to how we have been conditioned to respond to suffering and pain, through anger, denial, hostility and rejection.

As an alternative choice, the Buddhist path encourages us to follow the warrior heart in a different way by inspiring us to develop what is known in Buddhism as qualities of the heart as a way of living with suffering: (1) loving-kindness, (2) compassion, (3) sympathetic joy and (4) equanimity, not only towards others but also towards ourselves.

In this way, we learn to embrace the practice of love, compassion, sympathetic joy and equanimity as opposed to anger, denial, hostility and rejections. Now we will begin to have the tools we need not only to begin to heal our suffering, but we will also be better prepared and open to being of service to others. And it is in service to others that we heal ourselves.

As we can see, there is a place here for all of us on this path. There is a place for one who is wounded and for one who wishes to be a compassionate companion. This path will lead us all to the circle of healing, where we all sit side by side.

Native Inspiration

Wakan Tanka, Great Mystery
Teach me how to trust
My heart,
My mind,
My tuition,
My inner knowing,
The senses of my body
The blessings of my spirit
Teach me to trust these things
So that I may enter my Sacred Space
And love beyond my fear
And thus Walk in Balance
With the passing of each glorious sun

Lakota Prayer

Personal Notes:

Grace

Eight

SIGNS

Lost In Suffering ~ Loss of Self

It's a lonely world when we live in the midst of others and still feel that we are completely alone. When these conditions go on for too long, loneliness fosters deep psychological wounds that have the ability to color our thinking and our perceptions not only of others but ourselves. Isolation and loss close us in even during those fleeting moments when we desire to reach out; we remain frozen in time.

But in this space, we are not alone because our suffering, anguish and anxiety have been our companions all along. The whisper of the silence tries to block out the emotional difficulties that we find are too painful to bear.

When all we can hear is the roar of silence that fills our hearts and minds, and all we can think about is what we have lost, we remain adrift in our pain and sadness.

Still we know now that when we consistently hold back from extending our hand to others to ask for help, we are making the choice to contribute to our suffering and by doing so, we are unable to open our hearts, and our minds and we remain alone.

At the heart of it, as difficult as it is to comprehend, we do play a part in our unhappiness. We have a choice to do something different; we have a choice to be happy despite the history of our past. There is comfort in finally understanding that silence is our friend, and here in this sanctuary, we gather strength to move on when the heart calls for us to do so.

Out of necessity we develop coping patterns and routines that work for us, that help us find a way to get through each day. Too often we misunderstand pain and sorrow and think that our suffering is only real if others can understand that we are indeed struggling. Even if we do not have the words to tell them, we think that they should know. In this manner, we are unfair to compassionate companions and loved ones who genuinely want to understand, and we are unfair to ourselves by ensuring that we remain alone.

The pain and struggle that come with the suffering from personal traumatic events can be very subtle and lie sleeping beneath the surface for a very long time, almost feeling like a deep ache that never goes away. 'This' is suffering too, subtle, persistent and never-ending, but ever present in our hearts and minds, to the point where our spirit has simply become diminished.

Many will understand when we say that a tremendous amount of energy goes into 'discounting' our pain and struggles because we would rather struggle alone then even let one person with a kind heart and a strong shoulder be with us. But we can't begin to heal our pain and sorrow ourselves until we can acknowledge, even a little bit that something is going on.

Anyone who has been wounded or who has lived with trauma understands what it means to sense that 'something is going on.' Despite our most valiant efforts to remain in denial of our struggles, time after time we have learned that we can run but we cannot hide, clearly not from ourselves.

And so here at this moment we are ready to consider the question: What do we do now? What we can do now is to start to allow the sanctuary of silence to work for us, to begin to open our hearts to our voice, and to let the whispers begin.

It is not easy to open ourselves to feelings of discomfort and confusion; it takes a lot of courage to do so. But our voice is one that we cannot help but hear, and so we must choose to listen. Once we allow ourselves the ability to acknowledge some level of understanding, we then have the opportunity to begin to reconnect our thoughts and emotions that have been fragmented for such a long time.

Until now, our lives have been going in two different directions: one part of us is connected to the past and the other part of us cannot fully live in the present moment, because we have not understood that we need to relinquish the past to get to the present moment. When we do, we can start to change our perception of the experiences of grief, sadness and loneliness and begin to see them as our inner signs and messages, trying to find a way to tell us something that we need to know.

When we can quietly listen to our voice, perhaps we will hear the words *that it is time to go*. Both Native and Buddhist thought suggest that the act of letting go is the first step in the practice of acceptance, not wishing that things were different, not wishing that the past never happened, but instead accepting the past is how we learn to move on.

Monkey Mind

There are many complicated reasons that we feel held captive by our suffering, but one of the most noteworthy reasons is because of the mental Olympics that our minds engage in to avoid knowing what has already happened. Buddhist thought offers a kindly sympathetic view of the brain's behavior, and refers to it as 'Monkey Mind'.

Without even knowing the definition of Monkey Mind anyone that has ever struggled with thoughts that are all over the place, might already have a sense of what it means to have a monkey mind.

In Buddhism, this term is used to depict a troubled mind, one that is in a constant state of agitation and easily distracted. When our brain is endlessly in a state of discomfort and restlessness it cannot be happy, and if our mind is not capable of being happy, then neither are we. Perhaps this makes some sense?

Monkey Mind helps to distract us from the intensity of facts and recollections that we are trying to avoid, and while it might work for awhile, this is truly an exhausting roller coaster to be on. At some point, we realize that we need to get off of this exhausting ride. Monkey Mind does not create the problem but when the mind is out of balance and distracted, it does not help the problem. It simply makes it worse.

On a very basic level, the fact that we are struggling with Monkey Mind is a sign that we have lost the inner balance needed to handle our struggles, and that we are not in control, and internal control is necessary to help calm and quiet our mind.

We know that we cannot change what has already occurred and that we do not have the power to alter the circumstances of a traumatic incident, but we do have the ability to calm our thoughts about the incident and quiet the Monkey Mind.

We struggle with being hooked to the deep emotional attachments we have to past traumatic events. It is not to say that we intentionally want to stay attached, but merely an explanation that we have simply not been 'aware' of our inability to let go.

Many people might ask, "Why would anyone want to hold on to such memories?" It is not so much wanting to 'hold on' as it is being fearful that if we let go, we are minimizing what happened or that we are walking away from our wounded heart.

It is both complicated and utterly confusing that we appear unable to let go of something that we desperately need to surrender. Simply put, we are 'hooked' to the strong emotional attachments we have to the past. If we let go, what will happen to us? If we let go, are we saying the traumatic event never took place?

We are hooked on magical thinking that somehow we can change events that have already come to pass. This kind of thinking requires a great deal of negative energy anytime we try to change history and facts that cannot be altered.

Moments of Grace

Decisions for change come from within the heart and will only come in their own time. Our sense of awareness is instrumental in making a change, and as it increases so does our willingness to want to do something different.

The moment comes when it is no longer tolerable to simply be mindful that a traumatic event has happened. Now some decisions are needed.

With awareness comes a heightened sense of discomfort and agitation that become increasingly difficult to ignore. Until now we have been sick in heart, mind and spirit and these sensations and thoughts are our inner signs telling us that it is time to do something different about the way in which we have been living.

We are reminded that silence holds a sacred meaning in both the Native and Buddhist traditions and that silence is very powerful and to be respected. Silence is so powerful that given enough time, it can bring us to the moment of truth and realization. The understanding falls to us that we need to walk away from the path of resistance and instead, choose the path of peace, and walk away from the sorrow and indifference that we have been calling 'normal.'

We call this a 'Moment of Grace,' the unexpected moment

when something within quietly changes and triggers a transformation in our hearts. A moment of grace is when we quietly stay within the moment and acknowledge and accept our thoughts and feelings.

Within grace we quietly make the decision that we are ready to make changes to seek balance and harmony in our lives once again; we begin to look towards the journey of healing and recovery.

There is a long-standing belief in Native thinking that the majority of our sickness is the result of carrying unresolved anger and negative thoughts and feelings within us. By doing so, we create an unhealthy amount of negative energy within our mind, body and spirit. From a mind-body-spirit perspective, both Native and Buddhists thought understands this way of being as living an unhealthy life in every way possible.

It is believed, however, that we all possess the ability to change these patterns and to choose a healthy physical and spiritual life, as the balance between the two is essential to our mental-physical and spiritual well-being.

Seeking Recovery

The decision to seek recovery is one of the most empowering choices that we can make, and at the same time, one of the most difficult journeys we can make as it feels like a path of considerable uncertainty.

The beauty of the journey of recovery is that it is a lifelong process, one that we will explore and work with on a daily basis, as it becomes part of our lives and we become part of the journey.

Recovery does not insinuate beginning and end dates nor does it necessitate any labels. The journey of recovery honors and supports the yearning to regain homeostasis and balance in our lives. This journey supports the notion that we are all part of the human condition, it is understood that we will have both good days and bad days, perfection is not expected.

Some days we will move forward, and there will be other days when we will be drawn back to the emotional attachment to the past. This does not mean that we are trapped there; it does not imply that we have failed; it just means that we need to start again.

The beauty of this path is that the ebb and flow of the journey of recovery understands both our progress and our setbacks. This is what makes all of us members of the human condition, and in a sense it is what compels others to invite us to sit in the circle of healing side by side.

As we have noted earlier, Buddhism suggests a healing path that encourages the four qualities of the heart: (1) loving kindness, (2) sympathetic joy, (3) equanimity and perhaps the most powerful quality of all (4) compassion.

By embracing these qualities and by exchanging our negative thoughts and practices for positive ones, we begin to transform our mind-body and spirit; as we begin to feel the potential to regain a sense of ourselves and our lives, and we start to feel hopeful for a renewed future.

Of the four qualities noted above, equanimity might be the most challenging to understand, yet it has a central role in our journey to healing. On a simple level equanimity can be understood as a mind that is without hostility and one that does not engage in ill will towards others, but it is also important to note that this also implies no ill will towards the self, as we are so often our worst enemy.

A mind filled with equanimity is understood to be a peaceful mind connected to a strong sense of inner stability and calmness and one that can maintain balance even when experiencing difficulties, in many ways it is the antidote to the *Monkey Mind*.

In a remarkable way equanimity allows the mind to remain centered and balanced and by being able to look at the larger picture from a distance, it often protects us from being hooked and drawn back into negative thoughts and tendencies. Having resided in isolation and loneliness for so long, it often feels very overwhelming and frightening, when the moment presents itself when we decide to do something different.

After so much time feeling disconnected from others, we have a certain level of comfort with being alone, yet at the same time it is scary to think of making such significant changes all on our own. But it is not necessary for anyone to take these initial steps all alone when there are others who would welcome the opportunity to offer their silent support and companionship to be of service when one begins the journey.

Traditionally, journeys of recovery and healing typically involve the support of others. Often verbal support and guidance is frequently the norm. But it is also acknowledged and accepted that the spoken word is not always the first step chosen, but rather the willingness to simply sit with and listen to others.

Of the many paths that offer us support and guidance, both Native and Buddhists paths provide guidance and opportunities to help us all when choosing the journey of healing.

In many Native communities, this is known as the Red Road, a path that many choose when in search of the self while welcoming the guidance and companionship and wisdom of others.

In the same way, that Buddhism suggests the four qualities of the heart as guidance on this path, Native thinking encourages four additional qualities that support the journey of recovery on the Red Road: (1) Humbleness, (2) Respect, (3) Spirituality and (4) Truth.

When coming out of a prolonged period of darkness, it helps to be aware that a combination of the eight qualities that the Buddhist and Native ways suggest are some of the most helpful measures to assist in getting started on this transformational journey.

To those who would say: "This is too hard" or "I don't know how to start" or "I don't know where to start", or "I am afraid" it is important to remember that no one has to figure out these steps all on their own.

We should bear in mind that no one is ever called upon to walk the journey of recovery and healing alone. Perhaps difficult to accept, the beginning of the journey of recovery is illuminated with these powerful qualities, and it helps to remember that there are people who have gone before on this path, who are lighting the way. You are not alone.

Central to both Native and Buddhist practices are the importance of community and the concept of mutualism which is essential to the moral and social tapestry of both communities.

Mutualism promotes and encourages a sense of belonging within the community where all come together to work for the good of others; especially those that have lost their way, this is both the blessing and the handiwork of the circle of compassionate listeners.

From this perspective, it is understood that change or transformation comes directly from the heart and unfolds in its own time; patience and silence come together to give rise to the moment when change is chosen.

A Way to Change The Silence

Both the Buddhist and Native communities think of silence in both a noble and sacred way, and it is considered a blessing to be embraced by silence during the most painful of times.

Regardless of one's perception as wounded or companion, it is not difficult to understand that transformational changes that follow in the aftermath of great harm, are decisions that begin in the safety of the sanctuary of silence.

Our hearts are always speaking to us, but in the initial silence that follows traumatic incidents, it's hard for us to listen to our voice.

So often in the aftermath of trauma, we seek refuge in silence where we are once again struggling to find balance within ourselves. Unbeknownst to us, initially, the strength and truth that we find in silence eventually prepares us to be able to listen to our voice. It is here that we discover that if we can find a way to remain with a calm heart and mind in the face of the storm of sorrow, we will be able to regain our equilibrium, the balance of our mind-body and spirit.

Here in silence we find the strength to regain self-control, patience and tolerance, especially for ourselves. Silence strengthens the foundation of our character and our courageous heart and is the home of our ability to listen to our voices.

Silent words possess the power to resonate throughout our entire being as our ability to listen involves all of our senses. Sometimes the best way that we can prepare to hear both silent and verbal words are too quiet ourselves and in the silence simply give ourselves permission to just 'listen.'

It is in this quiet place that we begin to hear our voice, our words and start to learn to be with all of our pain and sorrow.

Look for the Signs

Where do we start? Once we begin to hear our voice again, how do we begin the journey of recovery? How do we begin to reconnect with ourselves and with others? Sometimes it is the small steps that help us to begin once we have chosen the journey of recovery to healing.

Native traditions offer us the chance to consider a path that is a spiritual way of life that is a deeply connected to Mother Earth. Within this worldview, we find absolute harmony with ourselves, our communities and nature that unifies the life force that we are all part of.

Within this tradition, Native teachings view Mother Earth as our universal mother and believe that we are all related to all other parts of Mother Nature, and as such we are all interconnected.

The many Creation Myths of Native American beliefs stress the interdependence between all people and all other forms of life. There is a feeling that the closer we physically stay to Mother Earth, the better off that we are with respect to keeping our spirits in balance.

During those times that we lose our way, it is a sign that our spirit is out of balance and desperately needs to find a way back home, as we remain disconnected from ourselves, from others and Mother Earth. At the risk of sounding simplistic, sometimes the first step forward to transformation and change, is just that, very simple, we have to start somewhere.

For those who feel lost, or disconnected, sometimes the simple act of sitting quietly upon the ground is very beneficial because of its quiet and serene nature, but you have to be willing to sit and stay awhile.

Many have shared that by simply sitting and taking our shoes off and placing our feet on the ground we can actually initiate the sense of the beginning of a reconnection to ourselves and Mother Earth. Simple? Yes, but it just might work. *(Go ahead and try it!)*

Each time we commit to reconnecting to Mother Earth, it serves to help us begin the process of reconnecting with our lost and unbalanced spirits. Once we are willing to listen to our own voice, we begin to feel a need to reconnect again, to move forward, to hear the voices of others. While the starting point is not the same for everyone, this just might be a beneficial way to set out on the journey of recovery and healing.

There are moments of grace in the aftermath of trauma, and we should be very careful to not miss them.

Native Inspiration

There is a road in the hearts of all of us
Hidden and seldom traveled
Which leads to an unknown sacred place

The old people came literally to love the soil
And they sat or reclined on the ground with the feeling
Of being close to a mothering power
Their teepees were built upon the earth
And their alters were made of earth
The soul was soothing, strengthening,
Cleansing and healing

That is why the old Indian still sits upon the earth
Instead of propping himself up and away
From its life giving forces
For him, to sit or lie upon the ground
Is to be able to think more deeply
And to feel more keenly
He can see more clearly into the mysteries of life
And come closer in kinship to other lives around him

Chief Luther Standing Bear

Part Four

RECOVERING

Emotional Healing

A collective mantra seemed to resonate throughout the 'None of the above' community that sounded something like this: "I have always admired survivors because they appear to have overcome the odds, but it does not feel right for me, it does not fit. Don't call me 'victimized' either, I am neither survivor or victimized, I see myself as wounded. So to me, every day is a journey, I think I will always be healing, always recovering. I am merely recovering."

Whispers

As If

As if in a dream
I sit looking forward and glancing back
Hearing the darkness whisper my name

My heart yearns to go forward into the light
Yet my spirit still calls to me to go back

And all this time later that goes from dark to light
I struggle to know which way I want to go

One side is where you are
And one side is where I am

This place where we were once side by side
Is now only
In a dream

Kc carterMartinez, Ed.D.

Personal Notes:

Faith

Nine

RECOVERY

Traveling the Windy Road

When traveling the road of recovery, it is essential to understand that recovery is a lifelong journey with many twists and turns along the way and not a destination. We should expect that there will be many stretches that will be a difficult road to navigate while there will be other stages of the journey that will feel much more manageable. It is a lifelong journey that can often appear to be tranquil, similar to the eye of the storm, but when we least expect it the road becomes complicated to navigate.

We should appreciate that the journey is ever changing, and while there are many moments of peace and tranquility, there will be moments of intense difficulty and sadness that we will need to embrace as we continue to move forward.

As difficult as it may be to fathom, once these internal transformational changes begin, we need to be open to facing the pain and fear that we have been hiding from, to break the grasp that the past has over us. Facing the pain is difficult for both the wounded and compassionate listener alike, as we all have moments in life that are so painful that we prefer to turn away rather than embrace them. We all know what it feels like to want to turn away from pain and sorrow.

By the same token, it is overwhelmingly painful as a compassionate, loved one to sit, listen and be with the pain and sorrow of someone we care for. As compassionate listeners, we innately understand that the only way for the journey of healing to begin requires facing the pain and going forward.

As tender as it is for the wounded to speak of their struggle, it is also heartbreaking for compassionate loved ones to hear the telling of a personal traumatic incident, especially for the first time.

When we love someone and hold them, dear, it is our hope that they will always be safe, and when our worldview is shattered, we find ourselves deeply distressed when we are faced with the reality that someone we care about has been in harm's way. Once we are aware that a personal traumatic incident has happened, we feel overwhelmed with a sense of heartbreak that we were not able to protect a loved one from such pain and trauma. This is emotionally devastating on every level.

Accepting Moments of Grace

We know that trauma does not care who we are, where we come from or what we do; trauma is the great equalizer to both the wounded and compassionate loved ones. As the wounded, one of the most difficult challenges we will ever face is to find the courage to look inside our own heart. At the same time, one of the most difficult challenges that we will ever face as compassionate listeners is to hear what is in the heart of a wounded loved one.

As the teller, it takes enormous courage and strength to be able to tell one's story. As the listener the same holds true, to be able to sit and listen to the story of pain and sorrow of a loved one is important. These are moments of grace; they are meant to rejuvenate us, inspire us and take us on the journey home together.

These quiet moments are rare to find in our daily lives. Because of our fast-paced lives and unforgiving, relentless schedules, we have lost the ability to simply pause, to take a moment and reflect. Most of the time we capitulate to incessant social pressure to move on and 'to forget' as if nothing has ever happened. And when these demands become a practice in our lives, our ability to recognize an opportunity that can bestow upon us a peaceful moment of quiet reflection often go unnoticed.

During these moments it is necessary to be still, to cease from moving 'away' from our discomfort and to simply be in the present moment. It is so easy to overlook these moments of grace, and if we do, we miss the opportunity to embrace the choice of recovery.

In what may seem like an unusual suggestion, we need to find a way to make friends with our fears and to face what is preventing us from living in this moment.

Both Buddhist and Native traditions encourage us to understand that the most helpful manner in which to respond to trauma and suffering is with empathy, kindness, and compassion. For the wounded, this is fundamental to acceptance and moving on in our life. But it also means that we must be able to show kindness to ourselves, the very thing that almost seems impossible to do.

Walking Away

To detach from our emotional attachments to the past, we need to bust loose from the beliefs that have taken up residence in our minds: (1) we are undeserving of kindness and empathy and (2) that once we tell our story, no one will want to be with us.

After all, who wants to be with a damaged broken person? We think back to the image we see of ourselves in the mirror, and this how we will continue to see ourselves until that moment when we choose to look away and instead look inward, where the authentic reflection of our experience can be found.

As an alternative to staring at this painful likeness, a moment of grace gives us the courage to pause just long enough to look away and look inward instead. The truth can hide in the shadows of pain and sorrow, but it cannot hide from the heart.

Once we take that step towards the journey of healing, that image will begin to fade away. Given enough time, we start to see our authentic image reflected in the eyes of our compassionate loved ones, a reflection that we have not seen for a very long time.

As compassionate listeners, when we are invited by the wounded to sit with them in the circle of healing, we are able to offer the companionship of someone to travel with and we are able to walk together within the circle of healing as they strive to find their voice and their way back home.

Walking along side by side, we are receptive to learning something from the traumatized that will enhance our understanding of what it means to live in the aftermath of trauma. At the same time, the wounded come to understand the importance of accepting the compassion, kindness, and support that we offer, perhaps for the very first time.

As compassionate listeners, we honor the words and stories of others by just listening and attending not only to the words that are spoken but to the life and emotions that the teller brings to us through their stories.

By attending to the words that are shared, we begin to understand just how powerful the spoken word is. However, this may be the first time that we are starting to realize how destructive and harmful the verbal assault of traumatic incident has been to those that have suffered a personal traumatic incident.

Words Hurt

So often when we try to visualize physical and sexual assaults, the images that come to mind are commonly physical ones, the images that most people associate with such events. But these images do not bring to light one of the most powerful invisible weapons of personal traumatic events, and that is the verbal assault that frequently accompanies many physical attacks, the hidden weapon of words.

Far to often words are used as mental and emotional weapons against the wounded, intended to demoralize, embarrass, humiliate and paralyze. While many may think that it is the physical aspect of such assaults that is so difficult to talk about, very often, the aftermath of the verbal dimension of assault, is even more haunting.

Words hurt. We know that personal traumatic incidents leave imprints on our mind-body- spirit and affect our ability to be present in our daily lives.

Words when intentionally used as weapons are distinctive, and unlike the physical elements of traumatic incidents that leave imprints on our inner world, the harm done by assaultive words, leave deep scars that are branded in our minds and on our spirits. These wounds are very much like a physical scar that fades over time but remains tender if not to our touch, to our memory of a tragic event.

From this viewpoint, we have a better understanding of why it is often so difficult for the wounded to talk about their experience immediately afterward. It is one thing to struggle with talking about the physical details of a personal traumatic event, but it is an entirely different circumstance when we understand how impossible and painful it is for anyone to speak of the verbal assault as it relates to the physical assault.

Words hurt. They stay with us. They do not leave. Assaultive words are intended to do harm, they are meant to break one down, and that they do. These are not words that can be easily spoken, repeated or shared, especially with a compassionate, loved one who only wants to help.

Sadly, they become part of who we are, and so often we let the words of that traumatic event define who we are as a reflection of our inability to separate our mind-body-spirit from the toxicity of the verbal assault.

Professional Listeners

Words hurt, but they can also heal. There are many professionals who have a passion for working within the field of trauma and healing. Many times, I have been blessed with remarkable opportunities to engage in in-depth conversations with respected colleagues from multiple disciplines. One such colleague was a female physician who possessed an unusually well-grounded compassionate and holistic philosophy and approach to trauma.

On more than one occasion these discussions came back to the problem of the relentless social pressure immediately after a personal traumatic event to divulge or to 'talk about what happened.'

Repeatedly she noted that in her professional opinion, this was considered 'insult to injury.' She felt that by insisting that the wounded provide a verbal account of the facts of the assault, only served to traumatize the injured all over again.

So often we would note, that the blunt statement of 'tell me what happened' emotionally traumatized the wounded all over again. Each of our conversations ended with the same thought; there had to be a better way to obtain information needed to provide assistance to the wounded.

In my work with law enforcement professionals, I discovered that these very same sentiments were shared by an investigator who specialized in crimes of violence against women.

In his opinion, the professional communities of both healthcare providers in the emergency room and law enforcement personnel needed to find another way to be able to talk with women who had been assaulted.

He too believed that the silence that immediately follows a personal traumatic event is very often misunderstood and perceived by multiple disciplines as a refusal to talk.

Over time, he made adjustments to his professional approach and reoriented himself to respond differently to crimes of violence against women, especially rape or sexual assault. He believed the same as the good physician, and I did, that verbalizing the phrase 'tell me what happened' only served to further traumatize the injured, and in his opinion, by making that statement was in fact: 'insult to injury'.

As an alternative, he modified both his perception and his approach and began to choose his words differently; instead, he would ask: 'What do you want to tell me' or 'What would you like me to know?'

At a time when the majority of investigators and law enforcement personnel who responded to crimes of violence against women were male, this investigator possessed both an empathetic and compassionate understanding of those who were wounded.

As a law enforcement professional, he is an extraordinary example of the healing power of professionalism, empathy and compassion. By the simple act of choosing to ask for information differently, allowed for the possibility of dialogue that might not have been possible under other circumstances.

This is both powerful and profound because it opens the possibility that the only difference between the traumatized getting help or not receiving assistance, is merely in the way that the information is asked. How many more traumatized women would be receptive to or able to accept help offered if the questions or statements were just worded in a more kind and compassionate way?

It had often been my hope that these two compassionate

professionals would cross paths, but that never happened. However, we all shared one common core belief, which was the use of the phrase 'tell me what happened', served to traumatize the wounded all over again.

They believed that words can hurt, so they found another way to ask for the information that they needed to be able to help, in a way that did not further traumatize the wounded.

Words hurt, but they can also show us a way back home. Our stories open our eyes and heart, very often it is how we use words that guide us on the road of recovery.

In moments of absolute quiet reflection, we will find that the words that we use to tell our stories help us to remember what we have forgotten.

At the right time, our words help us speak of our isolation, pain, and sorrow and to reach out and invite others to come and sit with us, so that we have the strength and courage to keep going on the road of recovery.

What Happens to Us

The fourth casualty of traumatic events is what we experience as collateral damage; the loss of others, of relationships and friendships as a direct result of the traumatic incident. These are not losses that we choose or that we initiate, but without question, they are the fallout of personal traumatic events that no one ever talks about. These are the losses of friends, loved ones and even professional relationships that we do not see coming.

Here again is another example of 'insult to injury' as we bear the burden of more sadness on top of the pain and sorrow that we are already carrying.

These are the some of the most grievous of losses, the ones that are too painful to talk about, often more so than the actual acts of traumatic events. They wound us to our very core and still they are rarely ever spoken about, sometimes never.

In the early phases of the aftermath of trauma, while

unable to talk about the incident to others, there are people in our lives that instinctively know that something has happened. While they may not know what has transpired, what they do know is that 'we seem different', and in truth, we are different.

For the wounded this is hard to deal with because so much energy and concentration goes into maintaining one's privacy. In our efforts to protect ourselves, from further harm or embarrassment, we are often unaware of how our altered attitude and behavior affects our relationships with others. While we may think that we are protecting others from unbearable information, our responses are changed in ways that perhaps only others can see.

Sadly, under these circumstances, many people naturally start to drift away out of frustration as the direct result of changes that they are unable to understand. In many ways this is like a pressure cooker situation, where the intensity of stress, anger and confusion keeps increasing and eventually something gives, quite often this involves walking away from the relationship.

Many people become impatient when trying to deal with changes in another person or a relationship, especially if they do not have any point of reference as to why things have changed. Eventually, in the absence of how and why chang-es have transpired, they begin to feel discarded and start to believe that the situation will not improve, and so they leave.

Collateral damage hurts. Without question, this is anoth-er form of 'insult to injury' when we suffer the assault at the hands of another and then must endure the unwanted changes that it has brought into our lives.

The loss of loved ones, people or relationships is like rubbing salt in an open wound, the pain reminds us that we are far from healing and that the aftermath of trauma continues to stay with us. These losses cut us to the very core as we experience their parting message as 'this is not mine to carry~ it is yours!'

We don't choose these losses; they come to us in the same way that the traumatic event happened to us, unwanted. The loss of those that we care about is very often beyond our control early on in the aftermath of trauma. Sadly, at this point, it is not easy to say which is harder to bear, the sense of the loss of self or the loss of others that we care about. For many, personal traumatic events foster a sense of being evicted from one's life.

In the aftermath of trauma, we find ourselves psychologically and emotionally frozen in our lives at the moment the traumatic incident is over. In the aftermath, we are consumed with an overwhelming feeling, that we do not belong with the people that we care for, and yet there is nowhere else to go.

In the wake of trauma, we find ourselves feeling disconnected in such a way that we no longer feel comfortable in our lives and relationships. And while we are unable to verbalize our experience and fears to others, frequently our friends and compassionate loved ones are unable to explain or verbalize the changes that they see in us and feel between us.

What We Do to Others

As we begin the journey of recovery to healing, it is critical that we understand that our compassionate listeners and loved ones should not be denied the opportunity to help us and to grieve with us.

Before the personal traumatic incident, we had a working appreciation of what healthy relationships look like, what they feel like and how they work. But in the aftermath of trauma, our sense of healthy relationships has become fragmented, and resultantly we begin to treat others in ways that we might not have before the traumatic incident.

In truth, this is unfair to those that care about us and by shutting them out we contribute to distancing ourselves from our loved ones. At some point, we need to realize that by isolating ourselves from others, we are choosing to disconnect from those that we care for. On many levels, we are unfair when we decide for others how they will feel or how they will think or act if and when we share our story with them.

As difficult as it is, as we move towards the road of recovery, it is crucial that we try to reconnect to our faith in our loved ones and trust in their love and faith in us, to simply be there for us, even at the end of our story.

What We Do to Ourselves

In our way, we play a role in contributing to the collateral damage that we experience after a traumatic event, and at a certain point, we need to take responsibility for that. As long as we continue to isolate and to shut others out, we guarantee that our suffering will continue, and so will the suffering of our loved ones.

When we decide for others what they can or cannot handle, we deprive ourselves of the opportunity to be heard, and to tell our story in the safety and companionship of those that genuinely love and care for us.

The longer we stay in isolation, the longer we are alone, but as we choose the road of recovery, we know, that this is a journey that we should not be taken alone. When seeking to heal we need the love and support of others, so perhaps this is the moment that we turn to our compassionate, loved ones, and say 'I have something to tell you, I am here, please don't leave me.'

Secrets vs. Privacy

Our social norms had changed so much from years ago when personal or family struggles were considered to be private. Conversations of a personal nature took place between trusted friends or between family members. You might remember the adage that was the universal mantra in most households: 'Don't air your family laundry', and everyone understood that to mean that family matters were not to be discussed outside of the family or the home.

For the most part, this is how people lived their lives, keeping personal matters private and not sharing or disclosing personal difficulties with others outside of one's circle of friends or family.

In the same way that there is respect for the role of silence, there was also enormous respect for privacy and for those that followed the social norms and showed consideration not only for their privacy but that of others.

Over the years, our social norms have deteriorated to the point where privacy is almost unheard of. In a strange twist of events, we seemingly have become a socially voyeuristic culture that exerts pressure on people to self-disclose personal matters that at another time would have been considered private. Gone are the days when personal difficulties were considered both private and sacred.

As a result, personal matters have become confusing for many people. We have social norms that do not differentiate between privacy and secrecy, and this confusion has the potential to exacerbate extremely painful situations.

When social norms recognized privacy as a personal right to be respected, it ensured that people were free from being disturbed or judged by other people. They were free from being pressured to share and disclose sensitive personal information, and at the very least, were guaranteed safety and privacy in their minds and homes.

The loss of these clear social standards has created cultural misperceptions on the concepts of privacy and secrecy. Far to often the option to maintain one's personal choice to embrace privacy is viewed as being intentionally secretive. Inferring the intentional choice to deliberately hide personal information.

For those that live in the aftermath of trauma, this type of confusion only makes the situation worse. Personal traumatic events embody an endless list of circumstances that suggest social explanations as to what has happened. But these circumstances are very, very personal and in the aftermath of trauma, tough to talk about and almost impossible to tell anyone else about.

This is a private matter and a most private experience that initially far exceeds anyone's ability to put into words; what we cannot say to ourselves, we cannot say to others.

We understand that there are both silent and spoken words and that silent words have an amazing ability to resonate through our entire being. While unheard by others, we can hear them, and until we reach that moment, that transitional moment when we choose to move forward, they will remain 'private' until we can share them with others.

It is a blessing that sitting beside us within the circle of healing, are compassionate listeners who have the wisdom and ability to understand the difference between privacy and secrecy, and accept without question the need to protect our privacy until we find our voice.

Collectively the circle of listeners surrounds us and keep us safe until we wish to speak, and as we know, that moment is a personal choice for all.

Ghost of the Mountain

When we make the choice to seek the road of recovery, in many ways, it is time to come out of the shadows that we have been hiding in. Seeking recovery means we are ready to begin to turn away from our inner time of isolation and turn outward towards the road that will bring us back into the light.

When we have been isolated for long periods of time, we tend to lose sight of others around us who are there to help and be supportive.

In many ways, we are similar to the legendary snow

leopard who secretly roams the mountains of central Asia. They are incredibly beautiful animals that are known to be shy, swift and silent as the falling snow and prefer to be alone.

Because of their solitary nonaggressive nature, they are rarely seen and often remain apart from the community that they belong to. They would rather be distant enough not to be seen, yet close enough to hear and see others in their community.

We are very much like the snow leopard, in needing to stay apart from others, but also wanting to stay just close enough so that others are aware that we are around. Like the snow leopard, we have the ability to keep our distance and at the same time as in the gift of the chameleon quietly blend into our surroundings, so that others might not be sure of where we are.

This is a way to be alone, yet not be alone, and it is an art that the snow leopard, also known as the *Ghost of the Mountain* has mastered. Because of their reclusive nature and inability to roar, it is often difficult to find them or to hear them. The members of their community recognize the puffing sound that they make, that signals while they are not visible, they are not far.

This is what we do, we try to maintain the solitary nature we embrace while in isolation, yet when ready to turn away from isolation and move towards others again, we need to find a way to let our voice be heard once again.

Both Buddhist and Native teachings remind us that we are all interconnected, and if we have lost our sense of connection to each other, we should remember that we are part of the larger community of Mother Earth.

When we are unable to connect to others, we may still be able to place our bare feet on the ground, to Mother Earth and begin to feel our reconnection to all that is around us. Much like the *Ghost of the Mountain*, when ready, we will reveal ourselves to those around us.

Native Inspiration

And while I stood there,
I saw more then I can tell,
And I understood more then I saw,
For I was seeing in a sacred manner
The shapes of things in the spirit,
And the shape of all shapes as they must,
Live together like one being.

Black Elk, Black Elk Speaks

Compassion

Ten

The Human Condition

Tapestry of Life

As we arrive at the beginning of the journey of recovery and healing, we harbor the belief that the image we have of ourselves is set in stone, and that there is no possible hope for change or renewal. There is this feeling that we are doomed to forever be what we have become, and that new beginnings are not for us. Part of feeling alone and isolated for so long has created this conflict mindset where we are unable to see any possibilities for change or light to guide us down the road.

Nevertheless, there is wisdom in the journey of recovery that defies this mindset, for within recovery we are afforded both the blessing and opportunity to redefine not only who we think we are, but who we want to be.

So often, in the early stages of recovery, we find ourselves confused, thinking that the purpose of the journey is to go in search of the person we once were before the personal traumatic event. Nothing could be further from the truth, for to go in search of someone who is no longer there, is simply tragic.

To do so, would be akin to chasing ghosts, fleeting

images that we see from time to time, but the haunting memory of who we once were, is lost to us forever. That person is gone, and instead of chasing after memories, we need to embrace the opportunity for transformation.

We have been given the chance to embrace change and to move in such a way that we no longer need to hold on to our tarnished image. Instead, we find ourselves willing to let go of this illusion as we walk towards our renewed selves.

Regardless of where we are on this journey, at some point we are all afraid, both wounded and listeners alike. As the wounded we cannot downheartedly stand by and accept this damaged version of ourselves; we need to want more; we need to chose to be in this moment, and relinquish the time of pain.

As a listener, we cannot hopelessly stand by and do nothing, because we cannot hide from the sad reality that we can see the pain, the struggle, and fear of others. We need to be fearless enough to extend our hand and say 'you do not belong here any longer', and to open our hearts and arms and say, 'come with me ~ it is time to go.' Here is the tapestry of our life, and we have the ability to make choices that will empower us to decide how our life is going to be!

Spiritual Warrior

No doubt, there will be obstacles along the way, but we need to hold on to the belief that we can regain spiritual balance and overall homeostasis. Both Buddhist & Native teachings remind us that the heart of the spiritual warrior which is within us all understands the struggle to let go of deep emotional habits that tie us to the past and accept the circumstances around us.

When we follow the path of the spiritual warrior we are reminded that our preoccupation with emotional turmoil has interfered with our ability to connect with others, resultantly we experience a loss of our close interpersonal relationships.

When we obsess about past events, we become self-protective and fixate about ourselves in such a way that we lose our awareness, compassion, and understanding for others. We find ourselves cut-off from the very people who are our lifelines back to mental-physical and spiritual balance, leaving us feeling isolated and misunderstood.

Even though our personal traumatic incidents on the surface, may look different from the suffering of others, all people within the circle of healing experience painful emotions, and unwanted circumstances. Even the tender-hearted can feel compassion for others, and we accept that some of the wounded may still need more time and privacy before starting out on this journey.

At the end of the day, we know that there may be some among us that ultimately wish to remain in anonymity, perhaps forever.

Both Buddhist & Native teachings suggest that if we want to quiet the judgmental voices that we hear in our hearts and minds, we need to embrace the practice of letting go. The key to renewed happiness and spiritual balance is through acceptance, which we achieve through the delicate practice of letting go.

By doing so, we consciously choose to turn away from the darkness that has kept us hidden from the light; acceptance is the cornerstone of the foundation of our renewed selves and a rekindled joyful life. That's right; you are deserving of a happy, balanced and joyful life. Take a moment to think about that.

We do so by trying to create a mind-body connection through a practice of mindfulness and reflections. To be in the present moment, by merely pausing to pay attention to our emotional reactions and the changes that these emotional responses bring about at any given moment.

What do we do when we experience certain emotions? Are there circumstances that trigger undeniable old emotional responses to injuries of the past? How many times are we willing to be subjected to the instant replay button to something that we can never change? How much time do you have left to squander on past struggles? How much time are you willing to take from your future?

Mindfully Letting Go

On a practical level, the practice of mindfulness and reflection compels that we naturally begin to consciously pay attention to the small details of our behaviors and reactions. How long are we willing to be held emotional hostage to an event in the past that cannot be changed? We cannot begin to change what we are not prepared for or willing to be aware of.

Mindfulness and reflection challenge us to stop being consumed by the details of the past and being drawn to the worries of the unknown future.

As difficult as it may be to believe, no matter how painful a personal traumatic incident has been, 'we' have the power to ameliorate our suffering by choosing to transform our frame of mind from a state of chronic anger and resentment to one of acceptance and peace. Imagine that.

Remember, we can never change the events of the past; they are over, immutable and unchangeable. However, we do have the power to affect a change in this present moment and our lives going forward, by choosing acceptance and letting go.

Many may help us along the way, but until we decide to relinquish the past and regain control over our choices, there is little anyone else can do to help us move forward.

It is our hope that through this practice, we will open our hearts to the kindness of others, and we will come to know how to show kindness not only to others but also to ourselves, an undertaking that feels almost impossible to many.

We Are More

As listeners, we understand that we all possess the ability to develop spiritual and emotional balance, but the journey begins with showing patience, compassion and kindness to ourselves first which then allows us to do so for others.

Mindfulness and focused attention are within our ability, wounded and listener alike. We all need to be able to express and receive loving acceptance in our efforts to reconnect with others, with those who sit in the circle of healing with us.

At the end of the day, there is a choice to be made: What are we going to do with this experience in our lives? Do we let it define us? Or are we going to embrace the opportunity for transformation and growth? What are you going to do?

Both Buddhist & Native teachings consider anger and other negative emotions as poisons, an affliction of the mind, body and spirit that will make us ill and unbalanced until we stop allowing them to reside in our hearts and minds. When we continue to do so, we remain spiritually bereft and unbalanced.

We have the opportunity to do something about this experience in our lives. We have the ability and the power to decide what we do next. We get to decide because we are more than the impaired aftermath of a personal traumatic event.

Here is a simple truth: either we make the choice to cope with our pain, anger and sorrow so that we can return to a healthy balanced life *or* if we do not, we will ultimately crumble and then it will deal with us.

When given the opportunity to take back control over our lives and our choices, we should never let that moment pass us by. The heart of the spiritual warrior that resides in each and every one of us, when acknowledged, will encourage us to be brave, and to embrace this opportunity and move forward!

The journey begins with the ties that bind each and every one of the threads of the human condition that connect us, one to the other. Whether we have had a particular experience or not, we have shared elements within the human condition that bind us together, even in the most difficult of times. So where do we start, how do we begin to come together for this journey?

The Ties That Bind

The tapestry of life that encircles us all is interweaved with distinctive threads of multiple colors and varying intensity. These threads represent the diverse emotional connections that bind us one to the other; thus, the ties that bind.

We all have a place in in the circle of healing, and as we sit side by side, we are linked together with the threads of emotional harmony.

We do not all experience or express all of the emotional elements of life's tapestry in the same way or with the same intensity. Our individual differences and the degree to which we feel connected to and part of the circle of healing influences how we express sympathy, compassion, self-compassion, and kindness.

It is helpful to think about the tapestry of life in the likeness of a hand-made patchwork quilt. While each quilt is different, each is made of patches of various sizes, shapes and colors that are all woven together to tell one story.

While most who see and touch the quilt will find it beautiful, each person may experience the quilt differently and not identify with every single patch or with all of the colors of stitches of the threads. But each in their own way can appreciate the beauty and uniqueness of the story that is being told, and at the same time be open to experiencing parts of the story that perhaps they were not prepared to see in the completed quilt.

As members of the circle of healing, we are very similar to the patchwork quilt. Sitting side by side, we all contribute a patchwork square to the story of the quilt as we each bring our experiences. Our compassion and support for others are evident in the colors of the threads that join all of the patches together.

Alone, we carry one voice, memory, and experience that is seemingly unique to ourselves. However, as we come to sit together, we bring the patches of our experiences to the circle to be intertwined with the others. Individually we stand alone, collectively together we create the tapestry of the patchwork quilt that holds us all together.

Somewhere in this quilt is a part of the story that resonates with us that will ultimately allow us to connect to others as we become more aware of the similarities that we share. In this way our hyper-vigilant awareness of how we are different from others begins to fade. Together we create the tapestry of the patchwork quilt that holds us all together.

Sympathy ~ Keeps a Little Distance

We begin with the thread of sympathy, the understanding between people that makes it possible for us to acknowledge and show a certain level of feelings of concern for others. Sympathy, while genuine, does not necessitate having shared the same experience or shared emotions. Sympathy is an unusual feeling, while genuine in nature, the mainstay of sympathy is to be able to express concern for another.

At the same time, there is a personal need to maintain some distance between oneself and the person in distress and their struggle. There is an underlying need to protect 'the self' and distance oneself from the other.

As in all interpersonal communication, body language and facial expressions conveyed out of sympathy suggest a concern for another, but quite often they do not display a deeper level of care for another.

We are all capable of experiencing and expressing sympathy towards another. However, those who struggle with the aftermath of a personal traumatic event are in need of a deeper genuine expression of concern. And as a listener we need to be able to express and connect on a deeper level than the simple expression of sympathy commonly allows for.

Sympathy usually involves keeping a little distance between the one who is struggling and the one who is trying to express concern. Sympathy in this instance, carries a suggested message that says 'I am sorry that you are suffering, but I don't want to get too close.'

At the same time, neither as the wounded or listener, are we here to judge the genuineness or quality of an emotional response from another. However, quite often when sympathy is the initial reaction to a complex traumatic event, the response suggests that the concerned person feels the need to keep one's distance. Frequently this discourages the wounded from feeling safe enough to let their guard down, and to welcome the concern.

Sadly, at this point in the aftermath of trauma, the wounded are too quick to accept this limited level of care, because 'we' do not want to get involved with ourselves, so it makes sense to us that 'others' prefer to keep their distance.

Because this is a time of intense vulnerability as both wounded and listener know only too well, there is a need for others to be willing to offer support on a deeper level, perhaps because this is the first emotional lifeline we might be prepared to grab hold of.

Of all of the varied reactions and responses to personal traumatic incidents, 'sympathy' is often the most difficult for the wounded to accept. While well intended, sometimes sympathy is experienced as one person feeling sorry for another, and as the wounded this is often negatively perceived.

Empathy ~ Comes a Little Closer

By envisioning our tapestry of life as a patchwork quilt, we can imagine the stories that each patchwork piece embodies within the large quilted cloth. Each square holds a separate meaning and tells a different story as it connects to the next piece, another part of the story.

The creation of the patchwork tapestry of life begins by telling our story one patchwork piece at a time. Each piece tells a different story as it connects to the next part, another part of the story.

If the expression of sympathy implies maintaining a little distance from those who are struggling, empathy provides a deeper level of emotional response to another.

The difference between sympathy and empathy is the ability of one to walk momentarily in the shoes of another to experience a genuine sense of the struggle of another. Instead of keeping one's distance, empathy offers the opportunity to be with one who is struggling through the sharing of wisdom and kindness.

The Three Threads of Empathy

Empathy is a complex emotion that is understood as having three different elements: cognitive empathy, emotional empathy, and empathic concern.

This perspective provides a framework for us from which to understand the different ways that empathy can be experienced or expressed.

Expressions of empathy emanate from a different emotional level, as those who can show empathy are capable of sharing and understanding the feelings, emotions and struggle of another.

Where the expression of sympathy is somewhat limited, those who express empathy function from the level of the heart and possess an ability experience what another is feeling.

Those who empathize do more than just listen to what is said, as they have the potential to experience the emotions that are expressed by the words spoken. Those who empathize respond from the heart, wherein they recognize others as equals and understand that the feelings, emotions, and experiences of another are just as important as their own.

However, we see ourselves, we all have the opportunity to respond to others with an empathic response by regarding the struggles of another with respect and compassion. From a cognitive empathy point of view, we have the ability to acknowledge what a person is saying about their pain, and we can empathize with the genuineness of their struggle. From within cognitive empathy, we have the ability to imagine the pain, sorrow, and struggle of another. The cognitive level alone does not mean that we will necessarily choose to take action to be helpful, but we do understand that someone else is indeed struggling and in need of kindness and support.

Emotional empathy adds another element of emotional response wherein we have the capacity to sense a physical response to what the other person is experiencing. In many ways, we can recognize and emotionally respond to the struggle of another.

Here, the feelings and struggles of another genuinely resonate with us. For some, this an intuitive response to the intensity of the physical, emotional or spiritual struggles of another.

Perhaps the deepest level of the expression of empathy is an empathic concern, which compels us to do more than just acknowledge the struggles of another. The ability to experience empathic concern urges us to show concern for someone who is in pain and struggling. Empathic concern drives us to 'do more' than just listen for at this level; the internal emotional response is to be of service.

The three threads of empathy strengthen the tapestry of the quilt and creates a long-awaited haven for the traumatized and nontraumatized to find a way to connect. Empathy forms a place of quiet reflection where thoughts and feelings can be expressed and shared, a necessary step in crossing the bridge that guides us all to the journey of recovery and healing.

The Compassionate Heart ~ Embraces

In Buddhist teachings, compassion is another form of empathy that comes from a place of truth, kindness, and sensitivity to all. Most importantly, real compassion is without judgment and arises when we see that another is suffering as we experience a deep, genuine need to do something, and to help in some way.

Both Buddhist & Native teachings suggest that the ability to experience and show compassion for others is a certain sign of a great compassionate heart towards others. On a symbolic level, compassion is evidence of our interconnectedness not only to each other but our physical and spiritual world.

Genuine expressions of compassion have the potential to create a sense of unity and closeness which speaks to a fundamental element of the human condition, that we are all interconnected and have a deep-seated need for acceptance and loving kindness from each other.

So often, we become consumed by our suffering, our pain, and sorrow and as a result, we become preoccupied and lose our awareness of others. Quite simply, we become lost. When we lose ourselves in our stories, we need someone to come and find us, someone to help us find our way back home.

Compassion means that we understand what it's like to be lost and to feel disconnected from others, so we stand ready to go in search of those who have lost their way. Compassion is about more than only caring about the struggles of another; real compassion means that we need to take action and become involved.

Part of the healing process involves changing our relationship with toxic and challenging emotions. When living in isolation, we are surrounded by these difficult emotions and find it challenging to see beyond them. After a while, when this is all we know, we feel hopeless and believe that there is no light at the end of the day. From within isolation and loneliness, we become disheartened and believe we are not worthy of genuine care or concern from others.

Empathy and compassion are needed for both the wounded and listeners alike as we walk the journey of recovery to healing. As listeners, we understand how necessary and powerful empathy and compassion are in the healing process.

Sitting in the Circle of Healing side by side, we lose sight of 'who' is the wounded or 'who' is the 'compassionate listener.' After a while we are naturally interwoven together and part of the community of healing. While compassion for all is offered and accepted, it is the wounded who struggle most with the idea of forgiveness and compassion.

As we travel the journey of recovery, as both wounded and compassionate listener, we have the potential and great heart to feel and show empathy and compassion to others and tend to do so without reservation. Part of being willing to show compassion to others is the challenge of understanding how important it is to be able to demonstrate compassion to oneself.

Self-Compassion ~ Be Kind to Yourself

Self-compassion is just as important as the ability and willingness to show compassion and understanding to others. Sadly when it comes to 'the self'; as the wounded we believe that we are not deserving of the same expression of compassion from others. But we have to ask ourselves, how can we care for others and show compassion for them if we cannot do the same for ourselves? How can we feel compassion for others if we cannot feel compassion for ourselves?

Regardless of how we see ourselves sitting in the circle of healing, these emotional responses are what is needed, not only to offer to others but also to ourselves. How can we help others if we are not ready to help ourselves? We repeatedly chastize ourselves for not 'knowing' when there was no way to know or for not doing something sooner to help; or for not preventing something we had no ability to prevent. How could we do any of these things if we simply did not know? How can we hold ourselves responsible?

Perhaps it is by helping others that we learn to appreciate that 'we' also need kindness and understanding? Maybe empathy and compassion for ourselves are learned in service and kindness to others? Is this another way of saying to ourselves 'Get out of the way!' How often do we stand in our way, resisting the spiritual call to be kind, accepting and compassionate to ourselves?

Self-compassion means we need to stop blaming ourselves for circumstances beyond our control; we need to stop criticizing and tearing ourselves down at every turn in the road. In this respect, we are our worst enemy as we continue to beat ourselves up with blame for a traumatic incident that we did not create nor have any control over. Ask yourself, why would you continue to blame yourself for events that are over? Why would anyone do this?

There is simplicity in the response to this question. No one wants to do this, so we need to stop our old behaviors, and we simply need to change. Self-Compassion is one of the many first-steps we take when we decide upon the journey of recovery and healing, but it is one of the most important ones. Because Self-Compassion involves 'accepting ourselves' as we are now and requires that we stop struggling to be someone we once were.

We simply need to get out of our way, because we have no choice but to start our journey from where we are. Wounded and listener alike: if we want to move forward, we simply need to make friends with who we are on the way to who we want to be. We need to release and accept the past and get on with it!

From the Buddhist & Native perspective, empathy and compassion are the beginning of the process to spiritual and emotional healing. The three threads of empathy are the multicolored strands that connect the patchwork pieces of our voices, stories and struggles together.

Compassion and self-compassion then are the strongest cords of all, as they bind all of the threads and pieces together into a compassionate patchwork quilt that encircles and protects us all, this is the tapestry of our story. The story told by the tapestry invites all to listen or to speak.

The Circle

The human condition calls us to come together in the circle of life. We all want to belong and to live a balanced life where we are at peace and can live in serene harmony with our loved ones. We all possess the ability to emerge from the suffering we have endured and reclaim the life we are capable of achieving. The more we yearn for a genuine peaceful heart, the greater our capacity for empathy and compassion for ourselves and others will be.

Traveling the journey of recovery and healing leads us to the Circle of Healing where all are welcome. Traditionally, the circle of healing is a group of people who gather together to sit in a circle with the clear intention of healing. Both Buddhist & Native teachings believe that the circle is a symbol of life's continuation, each circle being created for the purpose and support of the group.

While there are many meanings to the symbol of the circle, it is believed to be all-inclusive and represents enlightenment, strength, and the life cycle. Traditionally the circle has been the instrument that facilitates communication and strengthens and empowers the community members that sit side by side.

Within the circle, these compassionate listeners come together to create a safe sanctuary for all to come to and a haven for those that are ready to give a voice to their stories. As wisdom and courage leads us to the Circle of Healing where all are welcome.

The circle format offers new possibilities for a better understanding of self, others and the suffering at hand. In Buddhism, the circle is represented by two Kanji symbols that come together to form the Circle of Togetherness, and represent inclusion, wholeness and completion.

In Native American spirituality, the circle is sacred and a symbol of the great circle of life and it is within the circle that we find the center of our being. As with Buddhism, Native teachings show us the circle represents an opportunity for wellness and the chance to regain spiritual balance with the help and support of the community members.

From this perspective, the community comes together to help a member who has lost their way and is suffering, when the healing begins for the afflicted, so does healing for the community.

For each and every member of the Circle of Healing bring a piece of the patchwork quilt to the circle, a bit of wisdom, a piece of truth - maybe not very significant on its own, but when joined with the truth and knowledge of the others, is very healing medicine.

As members of the circle, wounded and compassionate listener alike, we understand that here in the circle we practice listening without reacting and without opinion. Instead, we refrain from negative influences that color our perspective. We listen with the beginners mind that allows us to be fully present in order to look deeper in search of helping the wounded.

As part of the community, we understand, that when one of our members are injured, as a community we are all wounded. Everything is an invitation to look deeper, sense more fully.

The power of a circle lies in our ability, to be honest with our thoughts and feelings and in our sincere effort to support others. The circle is an invitation to be part of the community and to help others. The strength of the circle is very powerful, and as we walk the journey of recovery and healing, others join us along the way, and the path widens to welcome more to sit in the circle.

Native Inspiration

Humankind has not woven the web of life
We are but one thread within it
Whatever we do to the web, we do to ourselves
All things are bound together
All things connect

Chief Seattle, 1854

Whisper

Follow the path of the healing journey for it is a linear circle
Remember you do not walk alone on this path
As we all walk side by side
Together we will follow the path of the linear circle
For it will bring us home to the circle of life
Let us begin the journey to healing

Kc carterMartinez, Ed.D.

Balance

Eleven

Getting Our House in Order

Life is a Linear Circle

Looking back, we remember when we thought that life
followed the direction of the picket fence, wanting to believe
that all the events in our lives happened in a particular order
and at a certain time. Somehow thinking that our worldview
determined what happened, and more importantly what did
not occur, essentially having complete faith that we had full
control over all aspects of our human condition.

As we begin our journey of recovery and healing, we
have a different perspective now as to when and how things
happen in our lives. We now have a deeper understanding and
respect for unexpected experiences and how unprepared we
are in the face of such happenings. Without hesitation, we can
say that having come face to face with trauma, we fully comprehend what a formidable adversary the aftermath of trauma
can be.

From within this new perspective, we realize that life is
not a picket fence at all, but a linear circle where life's events
do not happen in a longitudinal timeline, but randomly at

any given point within the circle. There is no order here, no pre-determined schedule of life events, just 'life' and all that it entails; that comes when it will.

Up until now, we have been dwelling in the shadows, and it has made us weary and doubtful for a renewed future. But now we believe that if we can have an open mind and heart, we will find the strength and courage to release the past and move towards our future, by embracing the present moment. It is quite simply, the time to get our house in order!

As we sit in the circle of healing with others, we come to understand that the journey of recovery and healing is indeed both a journey fraught with emotional turmoil and a peaceful transformational transition. When we least expect it, the aftermath of trauma will darken our path where once again we will feel as if we have lost our way. We need to be prepared for the unexpected challenges that trauma will hurl our way throughout the journey.

Trauma is transient and elusive, but it will always find us, and we should never lose sight of this. But we are stronger now and our resolve to remain present and regain balance in our lives is steadfast.

When the dark shadow of trauma comes to visit us, we should not be frightened or surprised. Instead, we should be prepared. From our place of renewed balance and harmony, we should make up our mind that when the aftermath of trauma reappears we will step aside and let it pass, just let it go by! Get out of the way!

Remember that if we can get out of our own way, the aftermath of trauma will pass through much quicker and not linger as long as it once did. In solitude we find answers that can help us change our lives, in unity, we find spiritual communion, courage, and compassion to go forward.

At the End of the Day

The aftermath of trauma is a consistent but elusive visitor that can surface at any given moment. Even when we have reestablished balance in our lives, an unexpected visit from trauma can turn our worlds upside down. And we might even feel as if we cannot hold on; that is unless we are prepared ahead of time.

Remember to be forewarned is to be forearmed. We need to remember that holding on for us is an indication of our determination to remain present in the moment that we are in, and reject the impulse to go backward.

At the end of the day, we have to be able to function efficiently to be able to do what needs to be done, to take care of ourselves, others and our lives.

Even on the best of days, this is not always an easy task, but on those days when we are facing emotional darkness, it is even more challenging.

We know that these troubling moments will come; therefore, it is imperative that we be prepared to meet these emotional challenges so that we can remain present and productive in our lives. You might be thinking, that is easier said then done, and you would be right.

Never the less at the end of the day we need to be able to perform the everyday logistics of our daily responsibilities. We have a responsibility to ourselves and to those that we love, to remain present with them, and we can't do that if we are continuously pulled into the past.

After all, who wants to be hanging around with someone who is not really 'here'? We all know what it is like to be sitting in front of someone who is looking right at us, but is clearly a million miles away in a place and time that we cannot go.

Time to Make a Plan

As such, this means that we need to have a plan. We need to understand that one of the fundamental ways that we face the challenge of dark days is to practice discipline as a part of our daily routine, not just during the difficult times.

Being prepared for difficult days is about much more than simply being able to pull it together on a bad day. It is about being able to master the emotional struggles that randomly find us in the middle of the day and it is about, being able to remain present exactly where we are.

As we travel the journey, we learn that being prepared is about changing the way we live each day of our lives, both peaceful and challenging. It is about making choices to be disciplined in a manner in which we chose to be present in our lives.

In the process of making choices, we begin to take responsibility for the changes that we want to make in our lives. We have to have a backup plan.

We need to have a different way of thinking. We need to have a different way of reacting to emotional stressors. We need to have a plan that will help us manage the dark moments that will come. And we need a plan that allows these visits to be just that, a passing moment.

Mindfulness invites us to pay attention on a regular basis in our everyday routines. Through mindfulness, we are encouraged to embrace a preference for discipline, which will help us stay focused in an open and mindful way despite difficulties.

By being disciplined in our attention, we are choosing a structured approach to staying focused on the present moment and a conscious decision to refrain from being drawn to old emotions, thoughts and behaviors.

But what happens when a dark day surfaces? What do we do when the dark feelings and thoughts that linger from the past still find us? The first thing that we do is to understand with absolute certainty that these moments will come. This is a given. We recognize this level of awareness as knowing; we know that sooner or later the aftermath of trauma is going to show up.

We resolve to be ready; we learn to be acutely mindful

that days like this will come and go. The hope being that with time, these moments will come less frequently, or that when they do we are better ready to manage them. Being ready means that we are aware and prepared for both the good days and the difficult ones. Our most essential challenge is to remain present in the moment. We do this by making a plan.

The Art of Discipline

Discipline and mindfulness are our most powerful allies for these challenges. The practice of mindfulness or 'paying attention' calls for a measure of self-control that assists us in being able to sit quietly with our thoughts and emotions.

Discipline is the fine art of making sure that we possess the ability to do what needs to be done, regardless of whatever mental, physical, emotional or spiritual turmoil we may be experiencing.

Ultimately this means finding a way to function even when we do not want to. It means finding a way to stay focused and to refrain from being pulled back into negative thinking and toxic emotions.

To do so, we need to have a game plan, a routine/schedule of structure and discipline that will help us sustain our strength and push through the emotional challenges and allow us to effectively function in the present moment.

Even on those days when we wake up and feel like the weight of the world is on our shoulders and we are wrapped in a cloak of emotional despair, we need a plan. In many ways, this is a practical matter that requires discipline, and a deep-seated belief that we can handle these transient emotional challenges.

Let's Get Practical

As we begin this part of our journey, it is relatively straight forward because, in order to get from one day to the next, we must simply be practical.

We know, that if we do not find a way to handle difficult emotions, emotional pain both past and present will cause us to not only hurt ourselves but others. How we handle difficult or painful emotions determines if we will be drawn into the web of the of the past, or if we will draw upon adequate plans to remain focused on the present. Our daily mantra at this point should be: we need to be practical!

One of the most uncomplicated steps that we can take in our efforts to be prepared is simple: *do something different.* We have to make a concerted effort not to fall back into the old patterns and behaviors that we are accustomed to and feel comfortable to us. We need to guard ourselves against the toxic feelings of comfort that old habits still hold.

We change our pattern of falling back into old thinking and behavior, by doing something different. Stop playing the instant replay button where we react and respond to both people and situations in the same way

Take a moment to think about how you felt when a bad day was upon you. What do you notice about your thinking? Do you feel like your thoughts are racing beyond your control? What do you notice about how you act? Do you think that you might become guarded around others? How do you feel physically? Do you feel tense, uptight as if your body is emotionally waiting for something to happen?

There are signs everywhere. Sit down and make a list of your signs. What do you experience when you know that an emotional storm is just around the corner?

We all know what it feels like to be on high alert. And when we remain on high alert for extended periods of time, we remain on guard towards our environment and everyone in it.

It is very accurate to say that when these signs start to surface, and the conditions of the perfect emotional storm come together, no one is safe from our volatile unexplained erratic emotions.

That is of course unless we make the brave decision to simply 'stop' instead of acting on these raw, challenging thoughts and behaviors.

What do we know about our old way of handling these awkward moments? We are aware by now that our old thinking and reactions do not work, other than to make a difficult time even more challenging. And if we keep doing the same things, then we will experience the same results. In this way, we continue to guarantee or suffering and the suffering of others around us.

Do Nothing ~ Just Stop

Without a doubt, it can be very challenging, even frightening, to let go of old patterns and behaviors, especially when they served a purpose for a long time. Sometimes it seems that we are just destined to grapple with our past struggles.

At the same time, it can be just as challenging to have to suddenly come up with new ways to manage old stuff. So what can we do? Nothing. We can do nothing. Just stop everything, take a mental and emotional break and simply do nothing! When we stop and do nothing, we are saying to the unwanted visitor 'not today, be on your way!'

What You Do 'Anyway'

Part of developing a practical plan requires creating a routine, a schedule that provides an outline and structure for what you expect of yourself every day. Schedules are our master plan for the day; they begin with the time that we get up and end at the time we go to sleep.

Some people do not like or need schedules and prefer to be free floaters, while this may work for others who have not experienced struggles with traumatic events, it does not work so well for those who have. Very often schedules or routines are what get us through the day.

At the best moments, we hope to be doing so well that we do not need a routine, but because of the transient visits of the aftermath of trauma, it is more realistic to have a plan in place.

Our routine or schedule is 'what we do anyway' regardless of what kind of day we are having, regardless of what transient emotional challenges we may be facing. The schedule defines what we do every single day, and it does not care what else is going one.

Routines and schedules provide time frames and structures that guide us through the day, especially on those difficult days, when we have lost our direction, as a result of internal emotional struggles. For our purposes, these schedules can be defined in two ways: (1) This is what I am doing today and the second one is: (2) This is what I am doing *anyway*.

This is not an occasion where we get to decide which one we want to pick because it is necessary to have both. In reality, the schedules are the same, the routine, the structure, the only thing that is different is the name of the plan.

The name of each schedule is a reflection of the type of day that we are having as well as the level of guidance and structure that we need to get through a challenging day.

It would be nice if every day on our journey were easy, but not every day will be. That is why the second title of this schedule: *This is what I am doing anyway* is so important because it is simply a concrete reminder and directive, that despite a dark day of challenges, we expect ourselves to do what needs to be done!

By adopting a schedule or routine it allows us to meet several goals in the face of difficult days: (1) To stay focused and remain present, (2) To do what needs to be done, (3) To step aside and let the aftermath of trauma pass us by and (4) To remain in the present moment and refrain from being drawn into the past.

The Powerful Three

The first three steps of any schedule I have ever made came from my maternal grandmother. She once told me that on those days that you decide that it is a bad day, that there is nothing you can do about it, that things will never change, and you are sitting there unable to get up and move, here are the first three steps that she shared with me: (1) Get out of bed (2) Brush your teeth (3) Wash your face. Then she would say, '*After* that then tell me how you are.' Powerful, practical and useful, you should try starting your schedule/routine with these three suggestions every single day!

Think About It

Remember when we discovered how powerful our thoughts are? When we learned that we are what we think we are? As we move through the journey of recovery and healing, this is crucial because our thinking affects what we do and how we are.

At this point in our journey, this is the time when we have the opportunity to change what we think about ourselves and to modify thought patterns and reactions that reinforce old beliefs about ourselves that are not true.

If we embrace this 'pause', we will be able to use this opportunity to choose a different way of living with our personal traumatic incidents.

As we begin this journey, this is the perfect time to think about what we do, how we do things and how we are not only to others but ourselves. Personal introspection is not easy, but in the calming quiet of a moment of pause, we can embrace the opportunity for change.

Native Inspiration

You must speak straight
So that your words
Go as sunlight into our hearts

Cochise~Chiricahua Chief

Personal Notes:

Twelve

PRACTICAL MAGIC

Practical Magic

Schedules and routines are great sources of support to get through a challenging time, and for the most part, they are very effective. There are times when we are suddenly faced with emotional struggles, which do not lend themselves well to the flow of our daily routine.

One of the benefits of daytime struggles is the physical presence of other people; this does not mean that just because others are around, that we will want to talk, but it does mean that it is often comforting to know that others are around.

Long-term exposure to isolation and loneliness make it difficult to break through the barrier that has been between us and others for a very long time, but in the early stages of our journey, at least we can see that others are around us.

A visual confirmation that we are not alone, regardless of how bad we feel, is at least calming to know others are around us, for when that moment should arise that we wish to connect with others.

The aftermath of trauma visits both day and night, in fact, it can settle in for prolonged periods of time. As such, the resources that we might rely on for the daytime struggles may not necessarily be an option, for evening or nighttime challenges. Anyone that has any experience at all with the aftermath of trauma, or loss or emotional struggles, know about the very insidious middle of the night battles.

Night time shadows show up at all hours of the darkness, like clockwork. They are the evening version of the aftermath of trauma, and in some ways, they are harder to avoid than daytime visitors because they are the thieves of the tranquility of sleep.

Anyone that has experienced night-time shadow visits knows that they come at all hours of the night, and they tend to stay, this makes for some very overwhelming and challenging nights. And anyone who has been up in the middle of the night knows, that the nighttime hours seem twice as long as the day ever does. This is a long time to feel isolated, alone and frightened, in fact it is more than most people can bear.

So we have to have an additional plan, more resources to lean on during the night time struggles. We should all understand that the journey of healing and recovery, means learning to live with and manage the night-time shadow battles that will appear.

The 20 Minute Rule

Our thoughts and emotions surface in response to certain situations, and environmental conditions that shake our memories loose, yet, there are times when they surface entirely independent of any external factors. They seemingly show up for no apparent reason what-so-ever, but when this happens in the middle of the night, we often feel as if there is no relief in sight, which can feel very frightening.

To intervene with night-time shadows, we fall back on the 20-minute rule; this means that we give night-time shadows only 20 minutes of our sleep, thoughts and our worry; then we need to do something different.

Anyone who has ever struggled with any form of trauma or loss knows what it feels like to abruptly wake up in the middle of the night as if someone had turned a spotlight on in your head! In many ways, this experience makes us feel haunted by our past traumas, and it is indeed a daunting feeling to think that things will never get any better.

A Native elder once told me that if you wake up in the middle of the night and cannot get back to sleep in twenty minutes or so, then get up. She said that we are awake because elusive thoughts and memories are traveling through our mind, and we need to get up and move around so that our mind can go back to sleep.

It is not that we do not want to go back to sleep, it is just that our mind is running on overload, and until we do something to shut our thinking down, we will remain awake.

So, we need to do something different, other than just stay there and wait for daylight to come. Get up!

Peaceful Environments

Practical magic involves schedules and routines and other hands-on interventions that will help quiet things down, but when it comes to night-time shadows, we have to find other things that will help. In the middle of the night, practical mindful actions lend themselves well to quieting the memories that are walking through our minds.

While there is nothing magical about these actions, they are practical, and instrumental in calming the mind that will not sleep. Practical mindful actions require a quiet, peaceful environment that works well with our efforts when trying to quite the mind.

When we transform our environment, we are able to intervene in a cycle that has our mind ill at ease. Start out by turning on a few soft lights, to create a soft glow in the room that you are in, because *soft* makes us want to slow down and relax.

If you have incense, place a few sticks of incense around the house to help create a peaceful atmosphere, but scented candles work just as well for many people. It is necessary to always keep scented candles or incense around as they are instrumental in the ritual of creating a safe and peaceful environment.

We can always change the environment that we are in, to reflect the level of calmness and serenity that we need to quiet the random thoughts and feelings that we are wrestling with. Once you are awake and up, it is important to be mindful of your setting, so be sure that you make the changes you need in your environment before you start any practical mindful action or task.

Remember that sound and lighting go together, when it comes to creating our peaceful environment. Some people prefer soft, quiet native flute music, chimes, piano, and yet there are others who get a calming feeling from having the TV on very softly in the background.

The manner in which we create a peaceful environment is a very personal and private matter, so it is important to take some time to determine what matters to us, what makes an environment peaceful for us, and ensure that we have what we need in our home to create this peaceful healing environment.

Practical Mindful Actions

One of the ways in which we are able to slow the mind down, is by using our hands. We use our hands to help slow our thoughts down and slow the cycle that our thoughts are locked in. There is something very healing and therapeutic about using our hands in practical mindful actions because there is a direct lifeline between our minds and our hands. When we are consumed by thoughts that we have difficulty letting go of, we don't seem to be able to think about anything else or focus on anything else.

Yet, when we start to do mindful actions with our hands, the very physical movement of any mindful action requires a certain level of attention, which allows us to become a little distracted from our relentless thoughts, when we start to focus on the physical motions of the mindful actions we are involved in; our thought process starts to slow down.

What kinds of practical mindful actions can we do in the middle of the night? There are a few, and they are very simple, the good news is that they help.

Dishes

Do the dishes! Fill the sink with warm soapy water and dishes, and while they are soaking, let your hands soak in the warm water before you start washing, just sit there awhile and let your hands absorb the warmth. If you are thinking that you don't have any dirty dishes at this hour of the night, don't worry about it, just put some clean ones in the water, it's not about dirty dishes, it's about you.

When you start washing, try to focus on only what your hands are doing, simply focus on the motion of your hands and how the warm water feels. The more you focus your attention on the task at hand, the greater chance there is to create a pause in the mind where the thoughts are running amuck, eventually distraction will slow your thoughts down. It follows that when we are able to slow our minds down, then our bodies will also slow down.

Sweeping the Floor

Sweeping the floor is therapeutic because of the repetitive physical action of sweeping. When we can't sleep we get caught up in thoughts we wish would go away, this type of concentration makes us feel very tense and uptight, so we have to do something to break that cycle.

The action of sweeping, by its very nature lulls the mind

into thinking that we are sweeping our troubled thoughts away, who knew? As in washing the dishes, repetitive mindful sweeping actions eventually calm the mind which in turn, allows the body to relax, begin to feel tired and encourages the mind to go to sleep.

There are two other household chores that possess unique calming features, and they are doing laundry and vacuuming. You might think this may seem a bit much for the middle of the night, but if these mindful activities can help quiet the mind so sleep is possible, it is surely worth the try.

Dryers and Laundry

When doing the laundry there is something about the hum and sound of the dryer that is magically soothing. The sound is like a hum that fills the room, and when you can sit and listen, eventually the humming sound and warmth of the dryer, begins to resonate through the body and calms the troubled mind. Depending on where your dryer is located, sometimes it is enough to do a load of laundry and then put it in the dryer and listen to the hum of the dryer as you try to go to sleep.

Dryers are magical in their healing abilities because the warmth of the hum can simply make both the mind and body relax, eventually sleep will follow. And if you need a little more time before going back to sleep, folding warm laundry is also very healing, soothing and therapeutic.

Vacuuming

Vacuuming is one more practical mindful activity that possesses another very therapeutic element because of the intense physical movements that vacuuming requires.

The magical connection here is the physical action combined with the sound of vacuum, which is very soothing and calming.

How many times have we seen the 'white noise' of the vacuum

calm an agitated baby? It works for us to, again, because, both the mind and body begin to relax, and the crisis of mind and spirit starts to quiet down.

Breathe In ~ Breathe Out

One of the keys to learning how to slow our minds down and to break the relentless cycles that our thoughts get locked into, is through our breathing. Through the breath, we are able to calm our minds, and break the cycle of repetitive thinking.

So often we think that it is the act of taking in a deep breath that is all that is needed to calm us down. On a simple level this is true, however, the real ability to calm our thoughts and quiet our minds and bodies, is directly related to when and how we breathe in and we breathe out.

Taking in a deep breath is helpful at any time, but if we really want to break a cycle of of relentless thoughts and worry we need to do a little bit more. We can certainly start with taking a very deep breath, but the secret is to do so very, very slowly. By doing so we are sending a message to our bodies and our minds, that it is time to take a break.

How often have you woken up in the middle of the night only to feel as if a bright light is on in your head, your body is tense all over, and you are hardly breathing? Being tense and uptight does not encourage relaxed breathing, instead we experience restricted and limited breathing that effects us from head to toe!

We cannot breathe out until we breathe in, and how we do that is very important. It is helpful to be sitting or standing still before taking a breath in. When you do, think 'posture' and be sitting or standing as straight as possible, then start to take in a very, very deep and slow breath.

Take your time, imagine that the breath is spreading slowly from the feet all the way to the top of the head.

Now think about it, if done appropriately, it should take a little bit of time to take the full deep breath in throughout our entire body. Once we have completed the breath, it is time to let it go, but very slowly.

Blow It Out Your Toes

When working with small children and adolescents who struggle with intense emotions and anxiety, we use an exercise called 'blow it out your toes.' The name alone has a funny tone to it and it makes you smile! A little bit of relaxation right there. The central idea behind 'blow it out your toes' also works with intervening with night shadows and thoughts that simply will not let go.

Once you take in a very deep breath hold it for a moment, before you start to release it and when you do, release your breath very, very slowly. We have a tendency when trying to calm down to quickly take in a deep breath, hold it and then release it as quickly as we can. But this is not an effective manner to use the breath to help us calm down and to quiet our thoughts.

The most effective way to use the breath to intervene with night time shadows is to release the breath as slowly as we can and for as long as we can. With children we use imagery of the breath as a colorful rainbow mist that we push through our body as slowly as we can, trying to control the release of breath until it has passed throughout our entire body. And just when we get to the end we push our breath out as slowly as we can and 'blow it out your toes'!

This takes a considerable amount of focused control and breathing to be able to finish with 'blow it out your toes'. However, when we are able to do so, it allows us to break the cycle of unwanted thoughts that are disturbing our sleep. It is not unusual to have to carry out this mindful practice several times before we begin to feel more relaxed and sense that our thoughts are beginning to calm down.

Children and adults alike, cannot help but smile when they realize that they have been able to control the remaining breath long enough to be able to 'blow it out your toes'! When properly practiced, the mindful act of breathing helps us to re-focus our thoughts, calm anxious feelings and settle our minds enough to return to sleep.

Who Is Your Person

Sometimes mindful activities alone are not enough to quiet the night time shadows. There are times when one of the most effective middle of the night interventions is to simply talk to someone.

This is often a challenge because most of us hesitate to call anyone in the middle of the night if we are having a difficult time. Yet, we all know, that there are times when having someone to actually call and talk to, in the middle of the night, is exactly what is needed.

So the question then is, 'who is your person'? Who can you call regardless of the hour during the night? It is not uncommon for many people to feel that there is absolutely no one that they would feel comfortable or safe calling in the middle of the night.

However, because of the nature of the aftermath of trauma and presence of night shadows, it is really important to identify one or two people who you can call 'your person'. Remember that we realize that there have been times that we have pushed our loved ones and friends away, not because of anything that they have said or done, but because of *what we decided* that they would think or how they would respond to our personal struggles.

Here is yet another example of a moment that we need to get out of our way. Make a *maybe list* of several people who might possibly be an option for you. It will take a little bit of courage, but you need to actually talk with each of these people and see if they are willing to be 'your person'.

Sometimes it is easier to find someone during the day, so it is critically important to ask a person if it would be ok if you called them in the middle of the night when you are experiencing a challenging night with night shadows. Just ask. That is all that you have to do.

Do not decide ahead of time what someone's answer will be, give them a chance to respond to your question, you might really be surprised at what you learn. This is difficult to take a leap of faith to give others a chance.

Widen the Path So That Others May Join

Part of being practical means that we take the initiative to be prepared for those times when our support plans and mindful actions might not work. What do you do if no one on your call list answers the phone? What if no one is available on any given night? Does that mean that there is no one to talk to? No, it does not, there is always someone to talk to, you just have to be sure that you have access to the correct information.

There are 24/7 crisis phone lines everywhere, and the job of the person who answers the phone is simply to listen and then to talk. All this means, is that you simply need someone to talk to and in the absence of any other resources, are using the 24/7 crisis lines in order to have someone to listen to you and have someone that you can talk to.

All communities have crisis lines, find out where one is in your community and make sure you have it posted in your own home, in case there is no one else to call. Perhaps the most important concept that we need to remember, is that the journey of recovery and healing is a lifelong process, where ever we go it goes, where ever it goes we go.

There will be many times that we cannot rely only on ourselves, and part of the journey of recovery and healing is realizing that it is alright to rely on others. At the same time, it is important to understand that we need to learn to lean on others when we are challenged and that we need to learn to let others lean on us.

The path to the journey of healing and recovery widens as we go along, allowing us to invite others to join us on the journey and sit with us in the Circle of Healing. We are not alone, there is always someone willing to walk with us or sit with us in the Circle of Healing, and perhaps more importantly, there is always someone else who needs to know that we are there for them.

Native Inspiration

Don't be afraid to cry
It will free your mind of sorrowful thoughts

Hopi

Part Five

VOICES

*T*his then is the first *telling*. The story that we first give a voice to. What we tell ourselves. Healing begins the first time we give a voice to our story. Perhaps this is when we embrace the journey of recovery and healing. Another first step. What are we able to tell ourselves? This comes first, before all else. How do we start? Where do we begin?

Trauma will always visit us. We need to remember this. Keep in mind that it is always transient. Like the shape shifter, trauma will come thinking that we are unaware, and like the chameleon it will try to disguise its intentions, thinking that we cannot sense its presence.

As we seek recovery, our mind-body and spirit are in balance now and for the first time in a long time, we are stronger then ever before.

Remember…

Remember, we have reclaimed our ability to make our choices once again.

Remember, we have regained our sense of 'self.' We know who we are.

Remember, we have rediscovered our voice, and we can hear our own words.

Remember, we have reconnected with our loved ones, and we are not alone.

Out of respect and honor for the voice of each story, the stories in Chapter 14 were kept in the format as presented by the tellers

Personal Notes:

Forgiveness

原谅

Thirteen

THE GREAT THAW

Signs That We Are Ready

So how do we know when it is time to move onward? For some, there may be a very clear moment when the choice is made, and the steps forward seem obvious. But for others, it takes some reflection to know when the moment has arrived.

Remember when we come out of a period of isolation we are just beginning to connect not only to others but our physical and spiritual connections as well. It takes some time to gain a sense of what is going on.

Native teachings have reminded us that we are part of a larger circle of the human condition, where people, nature, mother earth are all interconnected with each other. So in many ways, the signs that we are looking for, the clues that we are ready to go, may, in fact, be all around us, we simply need to be able to sit still long enough to see them.

Indigenous cultures around the world gauge their physical and spiritual life and traditions around the seasonal and physical changes of the place they call home.

By strengthening our ties to our environment, our

physical world and our emotional relationship with mother earth, we are better prepared to answer this question: How do we know that we are ready? Many of us live in the physical world that is governed by the four seasons; we recognize the changes that the seasonal shifts bring to each season and our lives.

Some Indigenous tribes live in climates where the elements are harder to live with, yet these Native communities have a deep understanding and respect of Mother Earth in the place that they call home. Native communities that live in the areas of the great ice have a deep respect for seasons of the ice and the changes that the seasons bring to them.

Here there is great significance and respect for what is called 'the season of the great thaw.' The power and importance of the great thaw are this: the great thaw only comes in its own time and at its pace. It cannot be forced, and it cannot be avoided, much the same as the sense of being frozen in time that the wounded experience in the aftermath of trauma.

Native community members respect and embrace the changes that seasonal shifts bring. They watch very carefully; they know they cannot rush these changes, so they listen, and they wait for a sign that the great thaw has begun. They know that they need to be prepared for the changes that are coming. The great thaw comes after an extended period of a deep freeze, which to the human eye can appear to be breathtaking.

The ability to listen is crucial at this time of the change as eventually, a subtle rumbling sound begins. Often people are not sure if they hear the subtle rumbling, but as they wait the sounds get louder and more consistent as it eventually turns into a continual loud roar. There is no way to escape Mother Earths voice as it eventually turns into a deafening roar that culminates in a thunderous cracking sound as if the ice is breaking, and that is exactly what has happened.

This subtle roar is a sign that the life below the surface is beginning to change. But since the great thaw comes from deep below it takes time to reach to the surface, where others can bear witness to it. The smooth mirror images start to shift as the sound gets louder, and cracks begin to appear across the surface, and finally the ice begins to break up.

The movement of the once still ice becomes swift, and when it starts, it cannot be stopped. It is impossible to ignore the raging silent roar that has been released with the cracking of the ice and as the water starts to break through, the fractured pieces of ice begin to move rapidly with the current away from the middle of the ice.

This is what comes about when the frozen connection between our brain – bodies and spirits starts to thaw – to heal – how do we know? Deep inside we feel a shift. There is a sense that we are starting to 'connect' again and that perhaps we no longer need to feel as disconnected from ourselves as we are beginning to feel the need to reach out to others.

This is the sign that we have been waiting for, maybe now that the great thaw has started we will be able to 'sit' for a short while, to take in thoughts, feelings, and memories that we have been protected from.

Like the ice that breaks off into different sizes and shapes, so do our memories and our recall. One part, one piece at a time. In the great thaw, it ebbs and flows, it starts and stops, and adjusts so that the shore can accommodate to the ice coming and going, once all is settled it will begin again.

When we can quietly sit with ourselves long enough to be mindful of this moment, the great thaw of our feelings, memories and emotions will begin, a little at a time.

As the current of the water starts to move it pulls the shattered pieces of ice along with it, the only sign that there is life deep below the surface, where no one can see it. Where once was a seemingly endless frozen glacier, the water, and the ice now comes together, gather strength and begin to move onward and outward.

Here is the moment that our journey to healing begins,

when we finally allow ourselves to hear the whisper of our voice and for the first time, we do not try to silence the sound. Instead we move with it and go towards it.

So we begin to embrace the journey of recovery and healing by walking together, by widening the path to invite others to join us and by sitting in the circle of healing together.

At the end of the day, this book was written to tell a story that would help us all understand that things are not always as they seem and that frequently something else is most likely going on.

That a person may behave as if they are feeling one way, and in fact are deeply feeling experiences that are beyond their ability to verbalize. That people struggle with more than we know, and they need our compassion and acceptance far more than our insensitivities.

That each and every one of us possesses all the empathy, compassion, and kindness that others need to find their way home again. That regardless of how we see ourselves as we sit in the Circle of Healing, others see who we are and remind us that we are never alone.

One way or the other we all know how painful it is to hide in the shadows because we are broken and feel alone. And because more than anything else we understand what it's like to deeply hurt for someone we care about and want nothing more than to help them find their way home.

In essence, we know that we are all part of the human condition understanding that collectively we are all part of the pain and of the healing and that the ties that bind hold us all together in the Circle of Healing. The simple truth is that all that is needed is for someone to say 'I am here and I am listening' and hold out our hand as an invitation to join us in the Circle of Healing.

Finally, and most importantly that we never need to ask the question, '*did this happen to you*' because the uncomplicated truth is, that the answer unequivocally just does not matter.

Native Inspiration

Seek wisdom, not knowledge
Knowledge is of the past
Wisdom is of the future

Lumbee

Tranquility

Fourteen

THE TELLING

Voice #1: My Story Will Not Define My Journey

My story is characterized by remnants of pain and confusion, remnants of sleepless nights filled with soul-gritting cries for the end. My story is characterized by repetitive cycles of highs (my motivation to find the purpose of all of my turmoil) and lows (being, empty, hopeless and dead in the inside).

My story is characterized by a cycle of normalcy, frequently interrupted by flashbacks of The nightmare from my past---flashbacks powerful enough to bring me to my knees, steel my Identity and cast a shadow of darkness over my life.

My story ended before it even began, between the ages of 3-7. My story ended when he Stole the light from my soul, took away my virtue, claimed my womanhood and destroyed my sense of trust in the world around me. Hate took shelter in my soul---I hated my body, because he was family...he will always be a part of me, genetically. I hate that he is still with me, that I 'may possess some of his physical characteristics, that I can't wash him away---that he will always be with me, all the days of my life.

BUT, my journey is characterized by a relentless hunger for survival, because like the Lotus, Permission Granted provided me with the tools that I needed to "renew and restore myself "time and time again." My journey is characterized by emotional bruises, tears and life setbacks because I will Always get back up. I get back up because I am at war with my story. Sure, I get tired of fighting---fighting who I should be-I should be sad, depressed, alone, Unemployed, single, an unstable mother, have low self-esteem, and the list goes on. But I fight for my life, my happiness, companionship, my family—I fight for the life I deserve. My story will not define my Journey!

Compassionate Anonymous Voice

Voice #2

He was the senior down the hall, a Jewish senior.

I was a *freshman, a Jewish freshman.*

He invited me over to his dorm the first night back of spring semester.

Because we dated, I felt safe with him, so I thought, even though I felt uneasy a few hours before I saw him.

While I was lying on his bed, **he** whispered in my ear that it would only go in half way.

I did not run away or make a move, even though I did not want to have sex with him.

He went in half way.

I woke up the next day, feeling like I needed to shower, needing to get this feeling off me.

In class I could not concentrate and felt like I was spiraling down and did not know who would catch me.

I blamed myself for what happened.

This did not happen violently I thought, like in the movies or what one would think of a rape scene. This was not 'violent,' yet I felt stripped of myself. I was just flabbergasted at what happened and how I felt.

I knew I had to do something.

I decided to talk with my friend in the lounge in my dorm and called my mom. I just remember tears were flowing down my face as I told her the story. I became angry and decided to tell the campus police. I decided to set up a meeting to talk with the Resident Director (RD) and my rapist about what happened.

I told him I felt **he** manipulated **me** and **I** told him he could not talk with me anymore.

Days went by and every time I saw a black and white coat in the dining hall or around campus I would think **he** was about to walk by or approach me. **I** did not understand why everyone else was so happy when I walked around campus.

I decided to open up to Dr. Kc a couple days after. She sat with me on a stairwell. We talked and she listened as I cried my eyes out feeling my world as I knew it disappear under me like quick sand. She listened and I felt safe with her.

Dr. Kc mentioned that there was a survivor club on campus for students who had gone through similar things as me. I brought one of my good friends to the club where we listened, shared and validated each other's experiences. We met women our age that had gone through experiences like ours and after that my friend and I became close with some of the other women in the group.

During the walk around town of night of Take Back the Night, we walked by the Girls Gone Wild bus and one of my good friends walked arm in arm with me as I cried feeling triggered by what I thought was going on in the Girls Gone Wild bus.

A month passed, and I decided to go on a date and thought I would be fine. When my date tried to kiss me in the movie theater I flinched, ducked and started to cry because I thought he was going to attack me, like the senior did. I was wrong. I was not okay. I apologized to him, told him what happened to me and he understood. I knew then, that this was still taking over my life, but in my mind I knew I was still a virgin. The senior could not take away *my virginity*.

I remember the day, 6 months later in the summer, when I decided to not let this rule my life and that this experience did not define me. This was something that happened to me and at that point I chose to not let these feelings and thoughts rule my life anymore.

When I would see the senior around campus and in the mall about a year after, I mustered up courage to wave to him. I do not like tension and I am the kind of person that will acknowledge you if you are in my presence.

I still wonder how he is doing and if he is doing what he wanted to do in life. I hope that he has learned how to treat women with respect. He was a part of my life and helped me learn how to take what happened to me and use it so I can relate to others who have experienced traumatic events in their life.

I do not wish this upon anyone, but I want to say "thank you," Jewish senior.

Compassionate Anonymous Voice

Voice #3

Blindsided. That's the first word that comes to mind when I think about what has happened to me. I have every other word to follow that most people in my shoes have: ashamed, scared, embarrassed, dirty, unlovable etc. I'm not sure there's a way to avoid any of those, but the first part was just blindsided.

I was 14 when we started 'dating'. I remember seeing him at school every day and smiling thinking that no one would ever be interested in me. A message that carried over from the years of being bullied. It was such a flattering and incredible moment when I was told by a friend that he was interested in me.

We started dating and we were the typical teenage couple. At first, everything was great, so in 'love' and didn't have a worry in the world. At the time I was a freshman and he was one year behind me.

The first two years were filled with traveling to each other's sporting events, spending time at each other's houses and with the families, the typical stuff.

He said all the right things that a young girl wants to hear from a guy. He did all the sweet things, like surprise flowers or walking me to dinner. I thought I had found this prince charming

As we continued to get older, all of our friends that were in relationships were starting to have sex and that started to come up in conversations. When I bashfully said I just wasn't ready, he assured me that I didn't need to do anything until I was ready and I believed him.

Junior year came around and all the girls in my class were getting ready for prom. The 'thing' to do was to go out to dinner with your date, for me, for me that was my boyfriend, then meet everyone for pictures. He had taken me out to dinner, just the two of us, and said he had a surprise for me at his house before he dropped me off at my house to finish getting ready for prom.

When we got to his house no one was home and he had taken me by the hand to his room. When he started to take off my clothes I hesitated and told him I still wasn't sure. He kept telling me it was okay, it was special and meant to happen for prom. To be honest, to this day I can't accurately tell you if I wanted that to happen or not, but maybe that says it all. I remember feeling uncomfortable, shy, self-conscious and scared. It hurt. I felt exposed. And confused.

From then on I was faced with a guy I didn't know. I went from dating someone I was head over heels for, to being in love with a guy I didn't know. After the night of prom, it was as if the boyfriend I had known disappeared. I felt broken.

Every day I was told that no one else would want me, that I was stupid, I wouldn't go far and I was provided a plan of what I would be doing once he graduated. He had told me where I would live, gave me permission to attend college but only under certain circumstances. I knew what kinds of dogs I would have and their names. Every aspect of my current and future life was controlled.

I spent two years being abused and assaulted. He would guilt me into sex--which now I know means I wasn't consenting. Statements like, "Doesn't my body tell you I missed you" or "You don't want to show me how much you love me?", were made constantly. I was programmed to respond how he wanted me to. I'd cry quiet tears and try to push him away- it didn't matter.

As if this was not enough, the constant verbal and mental abuse certainly added to it. My textbooks would be tossed across the room and I wasn't permitted to do my homework because it wouldn't matter I was "too stupid". Fun episodes of wrestling that left bruises down my spine. I had to hide from my family. I had to distance myself to comply with what he wanted and to hide from any questions.

Even though I was finally able to leave, my hell hadn't ended. I was so lost in my mind and heart. My sense of self was destroyed. I had no idea who I was or what I was worth. Honestly, I felt dirty, weak, and broken. Broken. I don't think I can say it enough.

The cycle of trauma doesn't end once you remove yourself from the traumatizing situation. The thoughts that follow, the beliefs of the world and of yourself, the flashbacks to those moments are what haunt you. For me, I landed in another unhealthy relationship because I couldn't see that I was basing what I felt I deserved off of the past.

It took me a year to utter any form of words that told my

mom what I had gone through. Now, I am stronger than ever and have used my trauma to teach me to help others. Do I wish it never happened? I guess that's a yes and a no. It destroyed me, but with time and support, I was able to turn it into an opportunity to understand others.

I carry the scars of a high school girl, a college woman, that has endured trauma that has taken control away from the one that robbed me of my innocence, my soul, my love of life, and belief in the good. I have those back again, but my fight isn't over.

Some of those fears and flashbacks stare me in the face; however, today I have a renewed strength to fight back and claim this life, this body, and this heart to be mine. Not theirs.

You do not own me. You do not control me. And you certainly have not left me broken.

Compassionate Anonymous Voice

Voice #4

I still can't say it out loud that I was raped. Not the best way of coping with the trauma but that was my only way. I denied it. Being born in a Muslim family I was too scared of the consequences. I didn't want my parents to feel my pain. I cried some nights and suppressed my emotions for years. It wasn't until I met some women who had gone through similar experience as me. For the first time that day in a room full of victims like me, I admitted that I was raped. I let this feeling in. It felt a burden lifted off my heart. I cried but that day I didn't cry alone. I shared my pain with people who cared, who were there to listen, to heal. A part of me wishes that I could go to my mother and tell her everything. But I know that it wouldn't change the history of my experience. It would only break her heart to know that I went through it alone.

Compassionate Anonymous Voice

Voice #5

If a stranger met me today, they would see a happy, energetic young woman in the prime of her life with a great job and a happy marriage. They would see someone accomplished with two Bachelor's degrees and a Master's degree, despite the fact that she was the first of her immediate family to get either. They would see someone who is passionate about her career. They would see someone who loves children and is excited to start a family of her own. But what a stranger may not realize is how much I have been through and overcome in order to reach this stage in my life.

Trauma does not always come in the form of just one single event. It can culminate in a whole number of ways. For me, it began in childhood with my mother being diagnosed with multiple diseases and receiving surgery after surgery, in order to save her life. Growing up, my mom was not able to carry me around or pick me up.

All of the love and sacrifice that my mother gave to me and my sister had to make up for the lack that we received from our father. On the days that my father was at work, I felt relieved, like a weight had been lifted off me. I was lucky.

My parents split up when I was around 13. It wasn't until I was an adult with a social work degree, working on child abuse cases that I found out the true extent of the problems between my dad and mother; the extent of the abuse that he made her suffer through. Things that if they weren't married at the time, any rational person would consider rape. But that is not my story to tell.

When I was a senior in high school, I reached a breaking point between all that I was dealing with regarding my mother's health problems and my father's abuse. My depression reached such a low that I would skip several meals at a time. I lost ten pounds in the matter of a week. I felt as though I lost the will to live. For a short period of time, I battled Anorexia Nervosa.

It was then that I met this guy at work. He was tall, extremely muscular and had the most beautiful blue eyes. He was three years older than me and in the coast guard. He had a career and his own apartment. This was extremely intriguing to a high school senior who just wanted to leave home and be considered an adult.

That boyfriend made me feel beautiful and special, two things that were very difficult for me to feel at the time. He would take me out to my favorite restaurants, cook for me, and show up to my work with Reese's Peanut Butter Cups because he knew they were my favorite.

One night, I went over to his apartment after work. We had only been dating for a couple of weeks so I wasn't ready to have sex with him because although I definitely liked him a lot, I knew I was not in love with him and I believed that sex was something you should only have with someone you love. But boy did I enjoy kissing him! The thing about this boyfriend was, although I really liked him a lot, he also scared me too.

One night, I was over at my boyfriend's house. I began kissing him however, he saw it as "teasing him." He told me "if you start it, I'm going to finish it." Next thing I knew, he was picking me up and bringing me to his bedroom. I told him no. I told him I wasn't ready to have sex with him, I just liked kissing him. Again, he told me "well you started it, so I'm going to finish it." I don't remember a ton about what happened next. I don't think it hurt, which is one reason that I was so confused at the time what to consider what happened to me. I just remember laying there and doing nothing. I couldn't possibly stop him, even if I wanted to. He weighed probably 150 pounds more than me in muscle weight alone. Plus, his temper terrified me. And the biggest reason, the thing that most confused me about what happened was, he was my boyfriend. I thought no one would possibly think that there was anything wrong with him having sex with me, even if I didn't really want to because he was my boyfriend. Plus, I was kissing him first. He even "warned" me that "if you start it, I will finish it" and I kissed him anyway

A few months later, I went to my gynecologist for my annual exam. I expected it to go smoothly, like all of my other exams. This time, I received a call from my doctor informing me that there were abnormalities with me pap smear. At this point, I was only 18 years old and this news was absolutely terrifying to me. What came next was a terribly painful test where my doctor had to cut some tissue samples from my cervix in order to test them. They came back as positive for the Human Papilloma Virus (HPV).

Not only did I need to process this news, I was still processing what happened with my ex-boyfriend. Never had I felt so violated in my life. Here, my boyfriend, a man that I'm supposed to be able to fall in love with and trust, has sex with me against my will. Then I find out that I have HPV because of having sex with him. Plus, on top of that, I'm having to endure terribly painful procedures in order to treat it.

Throughout the rest of high school and for the first couple of years of college, I really struggled emotionally. I went from relationship to relationship, hoping someone could fill this void that I felt in my heart. I couldn't talk about having HPV because whenever I did, my boyfriends blamed me for it and made me feel as though I were unclean. I felt as though I were Hester Prynne with a scarlet letter on my body.

Eventually, with the friends that I made in college and the Women Studies and Social Work classes that I took, I began to understand my emotions and the things that occurred in my past. I found a community of survivors; other women and men who had been through sexual assaults. I met others who witnessed domestic violence and had abusive fathers. I no longer felt alone. I began to heal.

Although college helped me heal, I still knew I needed

a life change. So I decided to leave; pack up my things and move somewhere where nobody knew me or my story and I could start completely over. I ended up accepting a position with an AmeriCorps program in West Virginia. I therefore spent a lot of time reading, hanging out with friends, and becoming reacquainted with myself. I began to realize that I deserved to be treated well and would only continue relationships and friendships with positive influences.

That year I also met my husband. I immediately felt safe with him. I felt like I could talk to him about anything and he wouldn't make me feel as though he were judging me. He also identified as a feminist and admired me for my degrees in Women Studies and Social Work.

He has never raised his voice at me or talked down to me in the nearly five years that we have been together. He has never called me a mean name, even in the heat of an argument. He values what I say and challenges me in my thinking. When I decided I wanted to go back to school for my Master's degree, he offered to have me move in with him and paid all of the bills so I wouldn't have to get a job while going to school, even though we weren't even engaged yet, let alone married at the time.

Leaving my home changed my life. At first I thought I was running away from my past. Now I understand I was actually running toward my future. Although life will always have its ups and downs, and I have been through my fair share as of late, I also know that I am a survivor. Not everyone wishes to be referred to as a survivor, but for me, with all that I have endured and am still able to see the best in people and in life, I don't know what better way to describe my life than surviving.

Everyone gets through their trauma in different ways. Some people need years of counseling and that is okay. I went to counseling at a few different points in my life. I think it's important to recognize when an event and the emotions attached to that event are too much to go through on your own and it is okay to admit that you need help.

Healing by one's self is extremely difficult. Although sometimes you may need to be left alone in order to process the things that are happening, and that is okay too. The emotions that a person goes through when processing trauma is a lot like being on a roller coaster. It is ever changing and one minute you may not want to talk to anyone and the next you might feel as though you'll explode if you don't talk to someone about what happened.

There is no perfect way to get through and process a traumatic event or experience. But I am here to tell you not to give up. No matter how low you feel, how hopeless the situation seems, you CAN get through it. The traumatic event you went through will never go away, and it's okay to still feel angry or hurt that it happened. But eventually you will be able to love again and laugh again and most importantly, live again. I know this because I have learned to live again and it's an absolutely beautiful life that I live and I believe that one day, you can learn to live again too.

~Compassionate Anonymous voice

Native Inspiration

Tell me and I'll forget
Show me and I may not remember
Involve me and I'll understand

Tribe Unknown

Serenity

Fifteen

AfterStory

Final Thoughts

These final thoughts found their way to paper while sitting in my favorite Laundromat. A place of quiet warmth with a calm sounding hum that you might miss if you weren't able to sit in silence. You would not hear the hum; you might not feel the warmth that fills the spirit and calms the mind and eases the heart.

In the course of these pages, we are transported from the moment that the traumatic event ends to that moment in time that we choose the journey of recovery and healing.

It has been said by many that it does not matter whether or not you have experienced a particular trauma, what is important is that we all know what it means to struggle with pain and sorrow, despair and confusion.

We all can listen; we can all offer support and open our hearts and our minds to those who choose to sit and walk with us.

At the end of the day, the details and the particulars are not what matter the most. What does matter, is that we are all here to walk this journey of healing together and to sit in the Circle of Healing side by side.

If you were to ask me, why did you write this book? In a quiet moment, I would respond as I always have, because I am a listener and a teller, it's what I am, and this is what I do.

And to my father and my husband who together spent years saying, write it down, I would say there is a time to listen and a time to tell, here is the telling.

Thank you both for being with me every single step of this journey, thank you for never letting go, for, without the both of you, there would be no journey, no story to tell.

Take your shoes off, sit down and put your feet on the ground, take a deep breath, clear your mind, open your heart and stay awhile. There is always room for one more in the Circle of Healing.

To all my Relations
Namaste sweet spirits
May you walk in peace

Buddhist quote

Our sorrows and wounds are healed only when we touch
them with compassion ~

Buddha

Gratitude

*H*ere at CheyWind Center for Trauma and Healing we express our heartfelt gratitude to the brave and courageous women who shared their voices here, some for the first time. Thank you for feeling safe enough in our Circle of Healing to give a voice to your stories. It is our hope that your voices inspire others to want to regain balance in their lives again. We know that your voices will inspire others to know, that there is always someone listening, there is always someone walking beside you and that you are never alone.

Namaste

Personal Notes:

Praise for Permission Granted

*P*ermission Granted: Journey from Trauma to Healing" is an inspirational and empathetic invitation to both the "traumatized" and to those who want to be "compassionate listeners" -- to reflect on the dynamics of the impact of a traumatic event. Dr. Kathleen carterMartinez creatively and skillfully uses the power of symbols to capture the essence of insights she generously shares in each book chapter.

The lotus flower, the cover on the book jacket symbolizes rebirth. Dr. carterMartinez also uses Chinese calligraphy, Native poetry, and songs that evoke feelings and images that characterize the healing journey.

Throughout "Permission Granted" Dr. carterMartinez expounds on the dynamics of a traumatized event and its aftermath-trauma. Drawing on her work in trauma she delves into the chaos and pain that goes with a traumatic event, and the role that silence and choices play in achieving homeostasis--a balanced body, mind, and spirit.

The most powerful message that Dr. carterMartinez underscores is the ability of each of us to control and monitor our thoughts. The insights shared by Dr. carterMartinez are applicable not only to women, but also to men, I strongly believe that "Permission Granted" is a book that will propel readers to willfully choose to leave a traumatic past behind, and, to take a healing journey to tomorrow

Linda A. Simunek, RN, PhD, JD

"I hold this book so close to my heart because the unique sense of belonging and community is indescribable. *Permission Granted* provides a voice to the victims of traumatic events, by validating their deepest thoughts and taking the reader on an individualized journey through personal trauma. *Permission Granted* provides a voice of patience, reassurance and education. As her words resonate from the pages and she guides her reader on a journey of mindfulness, Dr. Kathleen carterMartinez carefully crafts a place of safety, peace and rest---a place where victims of personal trauma can re-claim their sense of power and identity. This experience, unique to each reader, provides clarity to both the victims and the friends and loved ones of the victims of personal trauma.

Sherna Williams,
School Psychologist, M.A/C.A.S
Special Education Department Chair

Incredible! "Permission Granted" Is the ultimate guide to understanding the Human Condition. This book creates a safe; yet comfortable space where survivors can walk through the healing process of both the trauma & healing process. With "Permission Granted," Dr. Kathleen carterMartinez brings grace, innovation, & style to the Feminist Psychotherapy Community.

Denzell Green
Hip Hop Artist: Zooboy Yesterday

"Dr. Kc" speaks in a quiet and reassuring voice to illuminate the invisible nature of trauma. Her words offer insight into the nature of trauma, and how to cope and recover. For those suffering from trauma, and for those part of a support system, the gentleness of this prose will offer guidance, solace, compassion, and point the needle of the compass to the path of recovery.

Dr. Mark Taorimo

The lotus is known as the flower that rises out of the mud and still blooms with all its beauty. This perfectly opens Dr. carterMartinez' book that addresses the holistic realm of trauma. Trauma does not discriminate and through the sensitive, yet powerful words, Dr. carterMartinez draws us together to see how we are interconnected through our experiences. Through the chapters of this book, we can each grasp a new understanding of not only the experiences we or our loved ones have endured, but also how we can replenish our soul and rebuild our spirits while finding a new and stronger voice. Dr. carterMartinez demonstrates the depth of her compassion for those who have been through the whirlwind of trauma and uses her voice to teach others what is next – how we journey through the aftermath.

While trauma often creates a loss of hope and sense of fear, Dr. carterMartinez provides insight as to how to find yourself and heal through trauma. She has found those who were willing to share their voice to let us know we are not alone in this. We can rebuild ourselves and heal after some of the most painful experiences we have survived and we can help those we care about move forward as well. Our loved ones and ourselves can find tranquility once again. The words of Dr. carterMartinez will lead you through the journey and ease your soul into a healing nature.

Shanzy Carter-Martinez, MS, MHC, NCC

Whether it be a car accident, diagnosis of cancer, sexual assault, unexpected death of a loved one or domestic violence; most people have either been through some type of trauma themselves or know someone who has. "Permission Granted: Journey from Trauma to Healing" is a powerful book meant to explain the feelings associated with trauma and the process of overcoming it. This is a powerful and well-written book by Dr. Kathleen carterMartinez meant for any reader, whether you are reading to make sense of your own trauma or that of a loved one.

In her book, Dr. carterMartinez explains the difference between trauma and a traumatic event and also explains how the emotions related to experiencing trauma are similar to those that one goes through during the stages of grieving.

Dr. carterMartinez does a wonderful job of helping the reader make sense of the emotional journey that one goes through when processing a traumatic event and also helps explain it to those watching a loved one experiencing trauma. This is a book that anyone can read and relate to, whether you are an individual trying to make sense of your own emotions or a professional working in the field of trauma.

Emily Miller, MSW - Forensic Interviewer
Child Advocacy Center, Charlotte, North Carolina
Lincoln County Coalition Against Child Abuse

Permission Granted is one of those books that everyone should have on their bookshelf. This book will not only aid as a guide of self-healing, but also allow others to have a greater understanding of what so many people go through. So often, as a mental health professional and a human being, I have seen individuals hold back from speaking about traumas or showing vulnerability. By holding back, we are hiding our experience, and in essence prolonging the healing process. *Permission*

Granted is that permissive voice of healing. This book gives people the confidence to navigate their trauma at their own speed, make the choice to see ourselves how we want rather than how others choose to see us, and an understanding for those trying to help.

Dr. Kc utilizes her years of experience and innate understanding of the human condition to help others learn to rebuild. Her holistic approach makes each page welcoming and understandable to all readers. The inspirational tone in combination with quotes and poetry used by Dr. Kc makes this process possible. There is no pressure, no demands. She includes all aspects of the healing process and accounts for many different avenues one might take on their journey of healing. Those who read this book will find understanding, inspiration, and desire to navigate towards renewal.

Hollie Gibbons, M.S., NCC

Dr. Martinez has done a phenomenal job with this work, especially introducing the aspect of *We*. Far more often than not victims/survivors have to go along this journey feeling alone, depressed and guilty amongst a plethora of other feelings.

Yet Dr. Martinez has given readers whether a victim or not the insight on what it's like to lend a helping hand; even if there is nothing more you can do besides just being there to show support. I especially loved her analogy to the lotus because after reading one can only hope victims/ survivors all around can picture themselves as such. A beautiful being that even when you cast yourself from the world you still rise with your beauty once again. I like to think that the lotus sinking every night is compared to the struggles these victims/ survivors have to live with every day.

Her take on the different steps in healing and the difference between a traumatic event and trauma itself are truly enlightening.

All in all, I believe this is a great tool to use for anyone who have faced tough times as such and for the individuals around them. Even if you don't fall within these two categories it's still a great read with lots to learn from.

Corinthia Bell, M.S.

Through this intentionally-developed writing, Dr. carterMartinez helps readers explore the potential hope in life after living through trauma. Whether you are an individual who is or has experienced a life trauma, a family or a community, this book recognizes the emotional challenges that we may experience, and focuses on the meaningful healing process. Dr. carterMartinez shares the important notion that we each experience, respond and recover from trauma differently: our experience is personal, our own. This meaningful book challenges readers to reflect on who they want to be as a healing journey begins and strategies in working towards psychological and spiritual well-being. In a world where some readers may be feeling perpetual darkness, Dr. carterMartinez shines light on the movement forward.

Sarah Wild, M.S., NCC, Career Counselor

I'm not a big reader, but not only was "Permission Granted" easy to read, but its comforting tone provided an excellent attention grabbing philosophy. A philosophy that helped my often times overly-empathic mind deal with the idea of "trauma." I have felt the effects of trauma, and I've been in traumatizing experiences.

"Permission Granted" helped reassure me to "own" my trauma. "It's yours and no one else's." carterMartinez conveys a sense of comfort with the reassuring perspective of a human, experiencing the human condition.

A sense that "we're all in this together." From a methodically worded journey, to the inclusion of Oriental Calligraphy and Native American inspirational quotes throughout, we are taken for a ride on our own "emotional rollercoaster."

Whether we are the one's dealing with trauma, or we are comforting a friend in need, "Permission Granted" encourages empathic silence in a way that echoes Native Spiritual philosophies.

I now have a new found love and understanding of the silence, that is often prompted by a traumatic event.

But upon reading, I also understand the value of speaking about my trauma when I'm ready.

To my own experience, and also, the importance of words and thoughts I choose to describe the traumatic experience to myself and others. We're not alone in our grief and our pain and "Permission Granted" grants us the serenity of control, through silence and ownership of one's emotions, words and thoughts."

Jeremy Mathsen Creative Services Producer
WPTZ News, Channel 5/Plattsburgh, NY

Permission Granted is one of the most extraordinary books of our time that addresses the sensitivities of dealing with the traumas incurred by sexual assault, rape, and emotional abuse.

"Dr. KC's" invaluable insight offers guidance on a healing journey carefully designed to assist in attaining physical, emotional, and spiritual wellness in the aftermath of sexual assault or emotional abuse. Her ability to convey a sense of understanding and encouragement offers some of the most powerful healing powers to those who choose to journey with her.

Permission Granted is an invitation to participate in a warm, friendly, compassionate-filled healing journey with "Dr. KC" who deeply believes in the possibilities of overcoming the effects of sexual assault, rape, or emotional abuse.

"Dr. Kc" encourages a deeper dimension of healing from the effects of sexual assault, rape, or emotional abuse in *Permission Granted*

> *Linda S. Carpenter*
> *State University of New York @Plattsburgh*
> *Library and Information Services*
> *Classroom and Customer Support Services/Evening Supervisor*

Permission Granted is a powerful read for us all. Dr. Kc makes it clear that our worldview dramatically shifts when we experience a traumatic event. She explains that we all have to reflect and consider how we want to view ourselves after a traumatic event which may result in creating or choosing a new mindset in how we see ourselves.

In her book, she has intricately combined Native American poems and Oriental Calligraphy with her own thought - provoking poetry which provides a stepping stone for others.

This book can be extremely beneficial for individuals who have experienced traumatic events in their lives, professionals such as teachers, therapists, spiritual and religious leaders, and individuals such as a parent, sibling or friend who wish to help a loved one as we are all affected by trauma.

Dr. Kc beckons each and every one of us to consider the meaning and power of silence in a new light and urges each of us to embrace ourselves and each other to create a space where all stories are validated and silence is welcomed and accepted in voicing our experiences of the human condition.

Madeline Bogner, B.A.
Graduate Student

As a recent college graduate and social worker, *Permission Granted: The Journey from Trauma to Healing from Rape, Sexual Assault and Emotional Abuse,* was the perfect read for the work that I do. In the time that it took me to read this book, I have already picked up new ways to be a better listener and advocate for my clients. A brilliant piece of work by Dr. Kc!

Personally, I identified with so many themes in this book, I experienced several 'ah ha' moments while reading on the NYC subway.

I am recommending this book to anyone who has ever felt alone, invisible or scared to take the first steps of their own healing journey. I am proud to sit in the circle of compassionate listeners with the women and men just like myself who have experienced trauma and are finding their way.

Nichelle Llewellyn
Case Planner
Lower East Side Family Union
New York, NY

Kathleen carterMartinez, Ed.D.

Personal Notes:

Made in the USA
Lexington, KY
20 February 2018